CONCERT CHAMPÊTRE (PASTORAL MUSIC)　　GIORGIONE　　THE LOUVRE, PARIS

GIORGIONE DA CASTELFRANCO
PITTORE VINIZIANO

Line reproduction from the title page of
Vasari's Life of Giorgione, Edition of 1568

The Leadership of Giorgione

BY DUNCAN PHILLIPS ⸰ ⸰ WITH A NOTE BY H. G. DWIGHT

WASHINGTON: THE AMERICAN FEDERATION OF ARTS⸰ 1937

DESIGNED BY HARRY ROBERTS, JR.
PHOTO ENGRAVING BY THE BECK ENGRAVING CO.
BINDING BY FRANK J. HOWARD & CO.

COMPOSITION AND PRESSWORK BY
THE JOHN D. LUCAS PRINTING COMPANY, BALTIMORE & WASHINGTON

PRINTED IN U. S. A.

To

Marjorie Phillips

Preface

ANY book which aims to investigate a period of art history, even if its span was only a decade in one city, and which attempts to appraise the achievement of a great painter, even if scant records of his work remain, is bound to be a review of much that was written before. My debt to the scholars and critics who have preceded me in the study of Giorgione can only be suggested in the references and quotations of my text, footnotes and bibliography. I wish however to make special acknowledgment to Bernhard Berenson, Dean of the connoisseurs of the Italian Renaissance, who read an early manuscript I sent him and urged me to develop my theme. With Frank Jewett Mather, Jr., I have had constructive and stimulating conversations. His Giorgione differs from mine and his conception has been challenging. I wish to thank Will Hutchins and C. Law Watkins for translations from Italian and German authors and for never-failing encouragement. My book is honored and enriched by the commentary so kindly written for it at my request by the distinguished writer H. G. Dwight, now Assistant Director of the Frick Collection. The able and untiring cooperation of my associate Elmira Bier has helped me immeasurably with the index and with important details in the development of my project at every stage of its growth. I have been very fortunate in the sponsorship of the American Federation of Arts which undertook the publication and in the skilled and scholarly book designing of Harry Roberts.

To no one do I owe so much as to my wife Marjorie Phillips, a lyrical painter of today. Her inspiring comradeship in travel and her ever needed counsel and partnership in art have made the prolonged quest for a rare genius and a unique personality of long ago a profoundly delightful experience.

Acknowledgments are also due to Lord Duveen and to Colin Agnew. They supplied me with photographs and enabled me to see Venetian paintings in private collections. The American Magazine of Art has given me permission to reprint in a revised form an article which appeared in its pages. It is my hope that this volume, one of the first written in English for the general reader on Giorgione's art, will help clarify his mind and genius in a necessary comparison with the mind and genius of his follower Titian and to explain the mystery of his immortal fame based on so very few personally finished and definitely documented works.

D. P

Contents

Illustrations

Note on Giorgione

by
H. G. Dwight

AN over-documented republic takes care that those whom it delights to honor shall not lack a dossier. Handbooks record every step of a career. The newsreel and the press photographer familiarize a celebrated countenance. The movements and opinions of the great are served with the morning coffee. To us, accordingly, there is something unaccountable in the fact that so little is known of certain historic figures who do not appear to have foregone the precious boon of publicity. Among such figures Giorgione is one of the most baffling. Not only do the circumstances of his life exist largely in the domain of legend but the very paintings by which, after nearly five hundred years, he continues to be remembered. Of his two best-attested works, the Castelfranco Madonna can barely be called his, so often and so woefully has it been "restored," while time and weather long ago effaced all but a dubious shadow of the Fondaco dei Tedeschi frescoes. There remains a handful of widely scattered pictures over which no two amateurs agree. Certainly those accepted without question are excessively few in number; and there is little assurance that some unnoted parchment or some ingenious synthesis may not yet reduce the handful to limits still more melancholy.

For a man whose ruling passion in art is the great game of attributions, this is an intolerable state of affairs. If one is good for anything at all, reasons he, one should so systematically plumb a master of consequence, one should enter so intelligently into his spirit, one should so minutely observe his traits, habits, methods, all the ingredients of his style, as to recognize, no less infallibly than one recognizes the writing of an acquaintance, the work of his hand. Well, perhaps one should; but one does not—always. For there are admiring imitators, as there are crafty ones, who likewise seek to penetrate a spirit and a technique. Occasionally they come too near succeeding for our comfort. There are mannerisms which are not unique. There are even bad days or unsuccessful experiments. Then there is not only the fashion set by a reigning talent. There is such a thing as an artistic climate, which at a given moment may be prodigal of this or that outflowering.

⚹ ⚹ ⚹

Giorgione grew up in that heady Italian climate of the late fifteenth century which produced miracles without end. He and Titian and Michelangelo were born at what seems to us a short distance apart. Leonardo and Pinturicchio were then young men; Mantegna, Antonio

Pollaiuolo, Signorelli, Botticelli and Perugino were not old. Raphael was born within a decade of him, as were Lorenzo Lotto, Palma Vecchio, Sebastiano del Piombo, fifty other painters great or small. It was a time when everyone had talent and every Italian city put it to use. In Venice alone the workshops of the Bellini and the Vivarini, overwhelmed by orders, taught their craft to an amazing stream of apprentices. Giorgione, a pupil of Giovanni Bellini, holds among them all a place apart. He arrived late enough for the new technique of oils to have become familiar. He arrived not too soon to breathe that air of release from ancient conventions which reached Venice after it had stirred the more southerly cities into a ferment of new life. What there remains of Byzantine in the Castelfranco Madonna is modernized out of all resemblance to the Sacred Conversations of his master, with the slim girl and her baby seated high above the heads of St. Francis and a St. Liberalis who is an unadoring young knight of the period, the baby's eye caught by the gleam of his armour, his gonfalon tilted across just such a landscape as one sees in the hill country of the upper Veneto.

It is not as a religious painter that Giorgione is remembered so long—nor yet as a painter like Mantegna, who at thirteen watched Donatello at work in Padua and was forever haunted by something marmoreal in the design of a figure, by the order and measure of the antique. It is as the painter of certain musing portraits; of the mysterious little picture in Venice of a meeting by a river at the moment when a storm is ready to burst over the castellated town on the farther bank; of the delicious Music in the Fields, at the Louvre; of the lovely Sleeping Venus of Dresden (even if finished by another hand), in which the beauty and strangeness of the body, revealed after so many generations of sorrowful saints, is pure rejoicing of the eyes, untroubled by the suggestive unsaintliness of later painters. The High

Renaissance came to Venice with Giorgione, abroad in the morning of the newly recovered pagan world, no longer bound by hieratic traditions, free at last to explore the world flashing at the door, at last in consummate mastery of the pattern of a canvas, of the secret of recreating noble architecture with an illusion of reality, magnificent stuffs, a difficult attitude, a fugitive expression. We who weary of representation perhaps forget how novel an achievement that was. Yet with Giorgione it is not mere representation. It is something graver and more poetic. Whether he alone painted this or that we may never know. Still a portrait gracious and questioning beyond the ordinary, a figure of outlines neither metallic nor uncertain but suffused as it were in an afterglow of Arcady, a landscape transcending the romantic, at once dark and warm and magical, inevitably suggests Giorgione. He was one of the great innovators. But he fulfilled his destiny through those upon whom he cast his spell. He died early in his thirties, leaving behind him a golden legend and unfinished paintings that Titian inherited.

⌁ ⌁ ⌁

There is something both fitting and heartening in this book about Giorgione. Duncan Phillips is a critic and collector of and believer in what we call modern art. The phrase is deceptive because the unfolding present is a knife-edge of instability. What is modern today gives place tomorrow to something more modern still. What was modern yesterday often ceases to interest us. It must cease to interest us if behind it was nothing more than a juvenile contempt of bygones, an eagerness to be in fashion, a witless search for novelty. Yet it is equally foolish to walk with one's head over one's shoulder. Duncan Phillips makes neither mistake. Among his pictures are great bygones, reminders of the continuity of art, reminders of exacting disciplines. But he has the courage to take his chances with the present because what interests him is not chained to time. What interests him is the unquenchable impulse of creation. The painters of our day owe him an immense debt of gratitude. If the Venetians of the fifteenth century had been as preoccupied as the Americans of the twentieth with the painting of their forefathers, Bellini would never have had pupils to swell his own fame. The creative impulse, alas, is subject to moods. It burns low; it flickers desperately; it never quite dies out. And we never can foresee when it will flare up with renewed intensity, fed by what secret sources who shall say. Duncan Phillips is prophetically aware of that. He is aware, too, that the great innovators are not so sporadic as they seem. They do not spring by spontaneous generation out of the void. One secret source from which they draw life—witness Manet and his *Déjeuner sur l'Herbe*, derived from Giorgione's *Concert Champêtre*—is the immortal tree of art, with roots running deep into the centuries. So Duncan Phillips, friend of innovators, has had the intelligence to write this book.

The Leadership of Giorgione

The True Significance of Giorgione

Chapter One of
The Leadership of Giorgione

IORGIONE forged the link between his teacher Giovanni Bellini and his illustrious pupil Titian. More significant however than his acknowledged historical achievement in connecting two epochs of expert painting is the truth that he remained independent of both. It was his destiny to make a unique aesthetic contribution. He invented the painted lyric. As in the more abstract art of music the meaning reaches us subtly, through the senses, and the subject is almost inseparable from the picture form. Such a conception of art was far from general acceptance even in Giorgione's enlightened day. His was the prophetic kind of leadership which dares to stand alone. And this one can say about him in full knowledge of the fact that all too soon he attracted an infatuated personal following which included the usual standardizing and popularizing academicians. His own pupils were less like him than are the isolated lyricists of painting at work today. And yet, no matter how imperfectly he was understood by his contemporaries, he was certainly a source of immediate inspiration. It was only a beginning. There have been few precedents for individualistic invention in art quite so perennially inspiring as Giorgione's intimate, creative daring. His pictorial expressions of the elusive, the intangible, the otherwise inexpressible, are immortal for their own intrinsic worth. Nevertheless I wonder whether their greatest importance is not that they provided examples of a new kind of courageous, personal affirmation.

There seems to be no question at all that Giorgione's innovations of subject matter if not of style were extremely popular during his life. Such was the tolerant temper and the intellectual curiosity of his times that it is more questionable whether he would have had such success as came to him without his striving if his art had not really stood out for its nonconformity. During his last five years and all through the first quarter of the 16th century he was idolized not in spite of but actually because of his radical departures from the powerful Venetian tradition for painting. In its evolution from the stereotyped Byzantine it had advanced steadily yet not swiftly enough for the prevailing trend towards an informal and attractively approachable art. Although there must have been keen rivalry and even sharp antagonism between the old school and the new movement, this was modified by the reciprocity of respect and the probably affectionate relations which existed between the two leaders, old Giovanni Bellini and his best pupil, Giorgione. Their mutual understanding started from the hour when the brilliant boy of Castelfranco discovered the way he was born to go through the thrilling, mood-producing landscape backgrounds Bellini had painted as early as 1488. That was the approximate date of his *Transfiguration*, now in Naples, a picture which I love for its atmosphere of a clear, autumn afternoon in the mountains just before the sun goes down. It was, however, of the Uffizi Allegory, *The Infant Souls in Paradise*, that Bernhard Berenson must have been thinking when he wrote that the lyrical Bellini, indefinite in his subjects and not too noble to be charming, "could no more be translated into words than a sonata." The Bellini of the Allegory was the source of Giorgione's emotional landscapes. The younger man had merely to break with the ecclesiastical dogmas, the elaborated details and the divided interest between the figures and their background to which his teacher had remained faithful. Whether or not Bellini realized that the dogmas, details and divisions prevented

further development of free, imaginative composition and of functional, compact design, in any case he went forward just as far as he dared by pushing to its ultimate conclusion his own mastery of an all-pervading ruby or amber light as the criterion of a single dominant tone. He had carried his century as far as it could go with his fused and profoundly emotional color-atmosphere for the envelopment of his madonnas, saints and sacred stories. But that atmosphere of his was the only unifying element. The figures were neither affected by nor integrated with the more interesting and already more important landscapes. Other inhibitions persisted. New leadership was needed and wanted. A new age was about to be born. That there was no profound hostility, that there was, in fact, an admiring exchange of compliments between the Bellini academy and the young leader who seceded from it and set up his own more daringly progressive school, is evident enough from the first glimpse of the *Madonna* of San Zaccaria which shows clearly the influence of Giorgione's Bellinesque *Madonna of Castelfranco*, painted the year before. The Giorgionesque pictures by followers of Gianbellino confirm the impression that, first Lotto and Palma, and later, those more timid conservatives Basaiti and Catena, were encouraged by their master to join the circle of glamourous influence and to paint in that fresh springtime of sensibility which was Giorgione's gift to all the ages. Loyal as he was to prevailing standards and conventions Bellini was none the less the most open-minded and self-renewing of all the great artists of his kind. It was his own 15th century lyricism which had inspired the boy Giorgione to reverent emulation and the octogenarian

NAPLES

BELLINI

TRANSFIGURATION

urged his later pupils to pass beyond his own self-limited boundaries. His support and his ultimate conversion to a synthesis and suffusion of light, to a more enveloping kind of chiaroscuro and finally to secular and "Pagan" subjects made possible the victory of the modernists.

Giorgione never could have painted to please. In fact he may have been tempted many times to mystify the influential people who were so anxious to make him the fashion. And yet, it is true that he was one with his public in a tender sentiment for the pastoral poets and their Golden Age, that mental realm of pastoral pleasures and concerns, of leisurely day dreams and love affairs, of sensuousness without taint and of happy-hearted music-making. There was, for his purpose, the very essence of abstract art in the dreamy, distant view which generalizes and stylizes to the limit of heart's desire. In reading the bucolic fantasy of Theocritus and Virgil and the Arcadia of his contemporary Sannazaro the pleasure of Giorgio in the imagery must have become infused with a clear purpose to transpose such idylls into a pictorial and a plastic form. The pastoral word-patterns of Theocritus, so unlike the story-telling paintings of that best of scene painters, Carpaccio, were pure art, symbols of the spirit refreshed through the senses. The luminous Interiors, with engaging intimacies, auspiciously launched in Venice by Carpaccio in such lovable pictures as the *Dream of St. Ursula* and *St. Jerome in His Study* could evolve into really important subjective and expressive art if given greater breadth and unity of design and a true universality of appeal through the direct, plastic emotions. To combine a fantasy which was less of the literary than of the painter's imagination with a single-minded zeal

for a colorful and rich textured surface and for a personal and linear pattern, this became the central purpose of the young genius who dared to formulate what Vasari called "a more modern manner." Giorgione discovered for himself how to balance straight and curved lines and how to play with glowing lights and penetrable shadows in a musical rhythm. He knew that the rhythms of nature and the rhythms of life itself can be symbolized through the rhythms of art.

Consider the *Concert Champêtre* in Paris. I shall call it "Pastoral Music" to distinguish it from the *Concert* in Florence. There is the elemental abundance of nature in the earth-women and the intimate romance of art in the lute player and the relation of art to nature when each is well disposed to the other in the incident of the lutanist and his friend the shepherd tuning their instruments to their mutual satisfaction and in the intricately coordinated and absolutely inseparable relation of the figures to the landscape. Giorgione's conception was a dream of blended simplicity and subtlety, of simple country joys and subtle city culture unified in the fellowship of the necessary rhythms and an all embracing and enchanting light. At his death he left unfinished a pyramidal three-figure composition, the Pitti *Concert*, which conveyed a sense of the tantalizing impermanence of musical raptures and of the yearning loneliness of the soul, especially of the creative soul. These two masterpieces of painting, both inspired by music, are all we need to know of the mature Giorgione and his mind.

Such deep and serious thoughts of his must have been far from clear to unprepared observers of what, let us say to a gondolier, had appeared to be "Zorzon's" generally pleasure-loving and merely entertaining intentions. The Venetians were accustomed to be either instructed or entertained by their pictures. Since Giorgione was not instructive and since he was orthodox neither in art nor in theology then surely he must be chiefly an entertainer with his brush, even as he entertained his many friends with his lute and his songs. As to the poetic license of his drawing and the enigma of his subjects it is significant of the role he was destined to play, of his intervention for the sake of a free art, that the challenging aestheticism of his attitude had the opposite effect from what might well have been expected. Deliberately and with the aid of his caprice he underlined the comparative unimportance of subject, expecting, no doubt, to be disowned by the scholars and unpopular with the story-loving citizens. In every other period, and most of all under Democracies with their enlarged electorate, such would indeed have been his fate. But the ambiguity of his personages and their postures set the pedants guessing as to which Rabbinical, Hellenistic or Mediaeval legends he was illustrating. And the average citizens were in a mood to be pleasantly entertained by their own bewilderment. The biographer, Vasari, who was neither a scholar nor a critic but who had all the qualities of a good journalist, this barometer of a Vasari complained that he did not grasp the meaning of Giorgione's figures in fresco but whatever they meant they were distinguished and fascinating. That probably, was the reception to which Giorgione became accustomed during his life.

The first documents which throw any light upon the nation's reaction to his death were two letters dated only a short time after that event, to be exact, October 15th and 25th, 1510.[1] One was from that great lady and collector, the Marchioness of Mantua Isabella d'Este to her agent in Venice asking him to secure for her from Giorgione's studio a "nocte" characteristic of his aims in that it depicted a special condition of light. The other was the agent's answer. Whether the word "nocte" meant night scene with a St. Jerome or a Nativity with the pilgrim shepherds has never been decided but I am one of many who believe that Lord Allendale's *Adoration* in London is the picture Isabella had heard about and wished to possess. She certainly wanted an example of Giorgione which contained his unique difference from the "run of the mine" professional painters of the usual stock subjects. The agent replied that there were two versions of the picture she mentioned, one better than the other but both privately owned and the owners unwilling to sell. The letters reveal how much Giorgione's pictures were in demand in 1510, and how his new treatment of old subjects had led to commissions for variants like that less successful one of the two "noctes."[2] There is yet another inference to be drawn from the agent's report. Failing to get for the great lady the picture she wanted he recommended nothing else instead. Apparently there was little in the studio sufficiently far advanced to be attractive to collectors and such works as were finished, the *Pastoral Music*, for instance, were too new and daring in subject or, to be more exact, in lack of precise subject, to be desired by conservative patrons.

[1] The letters are preserved among the Gonzaga archives at Mantua. They are published in Archivio Storico dell 'Arte, Vol. I (1888), p. 47, A. Luzio-Archivist of Mantua.

[2] There is an inferior variant (a studio copy no doubt) to Lord Allendale's Adoration in the Museum Magazines at Vienna.

Isabella's keen interest in Giorgione's impressionistic luminism, however, is important evidence. Perhaps his studies of atmosphere with true aerial values and his symbolic arabesque of colors and lines were better understood by his intelligent patrons than by his followers and imitators. Perhaps Berenson was right in his early opinion[1] that "stirred with the enthusiasms of his own generation Giorgione painted pictures perfectly in touch with the ripened spirit of the Renaissance so that they succeeded as only those things succeed which simultaneously create a need and satisfy it." Certainly that great gentleman Baldassare Castiglione on May 23, 1524, wrote the following sentence:[2] "Here are those who in painting are the most excellent: Leonardo da Vinci, Mantegna, Raphael, Michaelangelo and George of Castelfranco. They all differ in their manners of execution . . . and each is recognized as the best in his own style." This passage is important, first, because the great arbiter of taste and learning, venturing to name the outstanding leaders and acknowledged giants of painting among his contemporary fellow countrymen as late as 1524, includes Giorgione but, strangely enough, neither Bellini nor Titian; second, because Castiglione's stress on the fact that each of his big men was unique "in his own manner" indicates the enlightened early Renaissance view of art that no one way is the only right way and that it is the duty and privilege of the connoisseur to appreciate each different manifestation of the creative genius at its best. It was Giorgione's good fortune to be born at precisely the right time and place.

His age was ready and waiting for his change of pace and for his epicurean philosophy. In a Venice where perpetual activity and costly material detail must have been overwhelming to sensitive, self-withdrawing individuals and when art was cluttered up with objective and imitative illusions and descriptive narratives while religion was dressed in sumptuous vestments and given over to ritual in gilded temples it is little wonder that there was a thrill in Giorgio's evocations of "the golden age" and of nature as larger and more enduring than man but of man as giving meaning to and drawing elements from nature. His few altar paintings and his soulful portraits, almost as generalized, those Heads, as his Theocritan pastorals and suggesting the mysteries of unspoken thought, were spiritually reassuring at a time when people realized that they were bustling about on perpetual dress parade. His distant forests, sunny glades and village glimpses, landscapes bred from bucolic fancy not from fact, offered vistas of escape to Venetians surfeited perhaps with their sumptuous architecture flooded by canal water. His courageous challenge to church and state that art and the human fancy could no longer be bound soon found a sympathetic response. Finally he struck the popular note with his celebration of a profitable leisure, a contemplative idleness in which the inner life was active and the mind mysteriously aware of itself. These innovations of Giorgione and of the partners who until 1515 completed or, in their own ways emulated his projects, transformed the art of painting from a public utility to a necessity of the individual. The simplicities and the subtleties of life were elusive and desirable in the Venice

[1]Bernhard Berenson: Italian Painters of the Renaissance.
[2]Codex. Ashburton Laurentian 409. It appeared four years later in the 1st edition of The Courtier. The dialogue is supposed to have taken place in 1507.

of pageantry and commerce. Giorgione was both simple and subtle.

I hope to make it clear that there was only one Giorgione and that the so-called Giorgionesque has been a delusion and a snare. There was a time when Giorgione's influence was supposed to have been so pervasive that it worked miracles and made little men great. How else could we explain that the *Concert Champêtre* was once given to the engraver and hack fresco painter Domenico Campagnola and by another expert to "a follower of Sebastiano del Piombo?" What absurdity! If these imitators ever borrowed their master's more daring technical idiosyncrasies the results were always lamentable. I am thinking of Campagnola's frescoes at Padua and of Sebastiano's in Rome.[1] Because of the sad aftermath of the bad and spurious Giorgionesque, his early death at the age of thirty-three was a calamity to art even though his true spirit endured and is still in the ascendant. The less serious immediate consequences of his interrupted projects have been my special study for this book. Since these consequences have to be apprehended through conjecture added to research I have no apologies for my hypothetical deductions, based as they are on a study of the artists as we know them in their most unquestioned creations. It is my conviction that the unfinished starts of pictures left in Giorgione's studio at his death were finished or retouched or, in a few cases, completely repainted by his closest associates and assistants. Titian was probably the executor who planned what to do or what not to do with the works Giorgione had started. To find traces of the creative artist himself and his innermost intention, if not his actual touch, under the changes which followed the taking over of the canvases by more obvious and explicit minds is a task which requires a thorough knowledge of all the facts, a familiarity with the individual mannerisms of the master and his pupils and an intuition as to the induplicable character of the creator's original purpose. The imagination must fill in with inference and hypothesis the gaps between the scraps of documentary evidence. I have pondered with never failing interest during the past twenty-five years the problems connected with the brief life of Giorgione and his unsigned, always disputed works. Such study is made difficult by two undeniable truths; first, that Giorgione has suffered more from the ravages of time and from the even more cruel changes wrought by insensitive and unskilled restorations than any other great master except Leonardo da Vinci; second, that he "left behind him" two collaborators, Titian and Sebastiano, who felt justified, since he had always welcomed their aid during his life, in carrying on his canvases after his death.

In the 17th century there was no capacity to understand the real Giorgione. While the demand for his work increased, a delusion as to what manner of man he was and a confusion as to what he had actually painted became a threat to his fame. Swept into a single heap labeled with his magic name and ready for much careless and unscrupulous exploitation were all the pictures of love-sick shepherds and their lasses, of lute-strumming gallants at the service of fair ladies, and, in general, all the story-telling pictures which were explicit and sentimental or the romanesque extravaganzas which were confused and chaotic in their mis-

[1]Scuola del Santo and Scuola del Carmine, Padua. Lunettes in Farnesina Palace, Rome.

reading of his abstract, musical intention. Giorgione has survived the imitations of Palma, Cariani, Bonifazio, Dosso Dossi, Romanino, Schiavone and the rest. We have come to recognize the qualitative difference between the Louvre masterpiece and the commercial derivations. Scientific analysis by Professor Morelli[1] and his disciples has made many of the earlier attributions ridiculous. Ever since Morelli the personality of the poet painter of Castelfranco has stood out vivid and consistent. He is no longer a legendary personage nor a name attached to romantic pictorial poetry. He is now the favorite study of the experts of the magnifying glass, the men who are wise in the lore of drawing, under painting, glazes and crackle and who expand or contract our prevailing conception of Giorgione's character and the scope of his creation according to their own daring or discretion. The problem is no less engrossing to the scholars who are best able to decipher the few old manuscripts and inscriptions which have added to our knowledge. I can definitely assure the reader of one truth. Many writers to the contrary, Giorgione was no myth. And his mystery is only the mystery of all genius. Now that we have scrutinized every picture and penetrated a few of them with the X-Rays and considered every reference in the archives Giorgione looms clearer than ever both as a man and as an artist. He was magnetic, original, independent, influential and all the while incomprehensible except to a few. He taught what he knew and he brought about a revolution in painting. And yet he was a solitary genius. Unmistakable for any other painter in spite of the collaborations which were practiced in his studio he was always true to himself. The mystery of his mind was made

almost impenetrable by the meddling of a lot of other men in his delicate self-expression. Most of the resulting mixtures are unsigned. Some of them were claimed by those who had collaborated or supplied "first aid." The followers with whom he is confused would almost seem to have tried their best to conceal the thoughts of their leader, a personality they did not understand. In spite of all this confusion Giorgione became the victim of a temporarily attuned but increasingly unintelligent public favour. Had he been less admired during his brief life and less desired by keen collectors his works would have been less tampered with by finishers and restorers immediately after his death. Fewer commissions would have come his way but this would have left him free to paint only such subjects as were of his own choice and these he would have done entirely with his own hand, with time enough at his disposal to make his methods and even his experiments sound and safe. Even then we might have had beautiful ruins like the *Christ and His Cross* in Venice, but at least there would not have been so many deadly repaintings of the *Madonna* of Castelfranco. If Giorgione was idolized from 1510 to 1515 for the right reasons it was inevitable, being what he was, that his cult would soon be carried on for reasons which right-minded lovers of his art must deplore. He had never really belonged to the many and the many will continue to rank him with the great for the wrong reasons. It is said that he is the typical romanticist of a romantic age and that he reflects in his subjects and in his point of view the Italian Renaissance. I have agreed with this opinion but only to the extent

[1]Morelli, Giovanni (Ivan Lermolieff) Italian Masters in European Galleries, 1880-86-91. 2 volumes.

of acknowledging that for a brief period he was what the matter of fact Venetians knew that they needed. He supplemented the tradition-bound painting of Venice with something more personal, more unconventional and in better taste. The familiar labels are misleading. He was in his age but not of it. Connoisseurs applauded him and society lionized him. Yet he would have been a fascinating stranger at any time, anywhere. And a certain witchery in his mind has no more to do with his exalted rank than the personal magnetism which Vasari recorded. In fact, his glamour and charm and the legends about his birth and his life have interfered always with an unbiased estimate and a sober analysis of his genius as an inventive painter and designer.

Of his historical function at least as the link between Bellini and Titian there can be general agreement. And even his more enchanted and understanding interpreters agree with the majority that for accurate draftsmanship, for thorough, realistic portraiture and for a technic in oils sound enough to make the surface safe he was inferior to the able and wise Bellini who formed him and to the even more skillful and resourceful Titian who for a time carried on his banner when he fell. Those two were the peaks of professional painting in their period. Giorgione was an uneven and to a certain extent a mannered executant. He had idiosyncrasies which no one can miss. There was the long, straight line almost invariably introduced as a diagonal. There was the leg of a seated figure drawn up at a sharply acute angle as in the young mother of the *Tempesta*, and the woman with the pipes who turns her back to us in the great picture at Paris. That supreme work, the *Pastoral Music* of the Louvre, may have faults

of drawing. In spite of them it is a masterpiece and one of the greatest pictures in the world. Instead of its being the inspiration of a brilliant boy, as Hourticq believes in attributing the work to Titian at twenty-one or two, I am certain that it is the intellectual consummation of a great man, Giorgione at thirty-three.[1] Had Titian conceived its mature subtlety of design in his early youth it would have been curious indeed that never again in all his long life would he quite recapture that inspirational unity between the landscape and the figures. The *Concert Champêtre* is the work of a man of completely matured genius, in the fullness of his powers. Fortunately, however, it contains also the fresh vision and the ecstasy of the painter's boyhood. Critics who apparently are unable to conceive of a genius which ripens rapidly have been giving away to Titian the works of Giorgione which surpass in scope, subtlety and plastic power his definitely authenticated early works. And yet the *Sleeping Venus* and the two *Concerts* of the Pitti and the Louvre must be the paintings to which Vasari referred when he wrote of Giorgione as the best painter of flesh tones in all Italy and of that change of style with increased powers of execution manifested by him after 1507.

Giorgione seems to me more important than either Bellini or Titian although he was less of a craftsman and less of an expert technician than they were at their best. He is not merely of Venice but of all the world. He is not only of his own time but of all time. He connected and transcended two traditions. These overlapped and merged four years after the date when he himself

[1] From a study of all the evidence I believe with Herbert Cook, Hourticq, and many others who have written on the problem that Titian was born as late as 1488-89.

grace for his complex subtlety of expression and his intrepid daring of design. I do not see him as a boyish page heralding the coming of a period of pomp and circumstance and of that virtuosity and power which Mather calls "athleticism in art" nor do I see him only as an attractive remnant of the chivalric Middle Age, as a wistful dreamer about old myths and poesies, as a sort of lute-strumming troubadour or backward-looking bard. I see in him the youth which recreates the world everywhere and always. He is the young artist of any age whose day-dreams are unforgotten but whose acute sense of opportunity, whose eagerness for new inventions, whose impatience to go forward gives the old world another chance to refresh its spirit and to alter its course. I see him as a primitive of what we call nowadays "modern painting" with special reference to its ever enlarged scope and its incessant research into new materials. Even if he is reduced to one picture, the *Thunderstorm* at Castelfranco, through lack of proof or a divided credit for the rest, or the ruin of other works which make their recognition difficult, even that one autographic creation

of his earlier years would cause him to live on as certainly the best of the Venetian pioneers of romanticism in painting; that transcendent glow of the mind which permeates and pervades subtly rhythmical and intimately personal patterns. We all know Pater's "momentary hint of stormy light which may invest a homely or familiar scene with a character drawn from the deep places of the imagination." When we come upon such a moment, such a particular effect in nature, we say that it is like a picture, like El Greco's *Storm Over Toledo* or Giorgione's *Storm Over Castelfranco*. In both cases nature was seen through a temperament. I am amazed how well the *Tempesta* keeps pace with our current æsthetic interests, especially in functional and unified structure and in the suggestion of "the stream of consciousness." Giorgione will always be a favorite of the few who, in every age and not merely in his own, cherish in life the memoried pause which is the music of fine moments. Walter Pater knew the spell; "an instrument sounded in the twilight as one passes through some unfamiliar room in a chance company."

What We Learn of Giorgione from Michiel and Vasari

Chapter Two of
The Leadership of Giorgione

Michiel used to be known as "L'anonimo di Morelli." His notebook dating from 1525-1575 was first published under the title "Notizie d' opere del disegno" in 1800. Edited by Jacopo Morelli (1884). ⟨First Edition of Vasari's Lives 1550. Second Edition 1568. English translation by Mrs. J. Foster 1850, used by Blashfield and Hopkins in their edition of Vasari's Lives 1896.

Vasari's short Life of Giorgione is the first and the best of the early biographies. Although he had only second-hand knowledge of his subject it is thought that his information was acquired from the artist's own pupils, Titian and Sebastiano del Piombo—with both of whom he had become well acquainted. Perhaps for that very reason his statements should be regarded as insufficiently detached and objective. Certainly he must be discounted because of the bias and prejudice he had picked up here and there concerning Venetian issues, the opinions which he seems to have been inclined to absorb too readily. Thus he underestimated Giovanni Bellini both as an artist and as an influence. This reflects the attitude of the generation of Venetians with whom he had talked, men who wished to be counted on the side of Titian and the new era rather than on the side of Bellini and tradition.

The late 15th century enjoyed the thought that Giorgione was the Venetian Leonardo and it spread the notion that if it had not been for Da Vinci's visit to Venice in 1500 Venetian painting would not have been awakened to striking effects of modelling with light and shade which, of course, became the stock in trade of its High Renaissance. Now it is true that Giorgione was affected by a new outlook, an experimental ardour, and this awakening came at an impressionable age when he stood at the threshold of his own career as an independent artist. Yet, his chiaroscuro became very different from that of Leonardo. He converted the black shadows into transparent and colorful ones and in this he had the inspiring precedent of his own teacher. It was Giovanni Bellini, that progressive patriarch and maestro of good painting who, after, approximately 1494, trained him and gave him his start as a colorist and as a lyricist of light.

Giorgione was born at Castelfranco in 1477. The 17th century legend that he was the natural son of a nobleman of the house of Barbarella and a peasant girl from the neighboring village of Vedelago has long ago been discredited as a fictitious prop to the evidently widespread comparison of the Venetian leader with Leonardo and his illegitimate birth. Ridolfi in 1648 had called him Giorgio Barbarelli which may have authorized the fable but in the older manuscripts the name we come upon is not even the abbreviated Giorgio but the nicknames of Zorzon or Zorzi. Vasari explains that the painter came to be known as Giorgione, which means "Great George" because of his impressive physical stature and the distinction of his mind and talent but Dr. Gronau has traced him back to his father or grandfather Giorgione da Vedelago who was a resident of Castelfranco in 1460. Although Vasari claimed that he was of humble birth Carlo Ridolfi[1] states that he belonged to an old and distinguished family and he certainly revealed many qualities associated with innate refinement. Yet, Vasari was more probably right. We know from Ridolfi's book and from an early 18th century manuscript found at Castelfranco written by a native called Melchiori[2] that Zorzon was honored by the great General Tuzio Constanzo. It was also Ridolfi who made the earliest reference to the Madonna with St. Francis and St. Liberale which he said was painted on a commission for the parish church and bore the Constanza coat of arms. Melchiori, recording the history of this great family, tells of the death of Tuzio's second son Mathieu, near Ravenna in 1504 at the age of 23 (when Giorgione was 27) while in command of a company of lances, also of his burial in a chapel

MATHEUS CONSTANTIUS   PRIVATE COLLECTION, PARIS
Attributed to GIORGIONE
The attribution by Hourticq is based on a facial resemblance to the S. Liberale of Castelfranco

of the church at Castelfranco where he is commemorated both in sculpture and painting and represented in full armour. Louis Hourticq has discovered in a private collection in Paris[3] a portrait of a young man bearing the inscription "Matheus Constantius." The large eyes and small mouth recall the S. Liberale of Giorgione's *Madonna*. This, of course, may not be by the master himself. Having been unable to see the picture I am as yet unqualified to express an opinion. But whether or not Giorgio painted his head several years earlier and had, therefore, known him in early manhood, the fact that he

[1] "Le Maraviglie dell'arte della Pittura" 1648.
[2] Melchiori, Natale "Cronaca di Castelfranco 1724" Museo Avico, Venice.
[3] Collection of H. Gentili di Giuseppe, Paris.

was honored by the father of the young soldier makes it plausible that he was a boyhood friend of the hero and that he drew his features under the helmet of the warrior saint.

Giorgio might well have received his earliest training in the town of Bassano, eight miles from his home, and returned often to Castelfranco during his art education in Venice. Yet, he must have been still a boy when, let us say, about 1494, he entered the school of Giovanni Bellini as a pupil and studio assistant. He became very popular, says Vasari, for his many accomplishments and his personal magnetism. Seeking for ways to pad insufficient knowledge of this foreigner (a foreigner our poet-painter always was even in Venice) the biographer related what his friend Sebastiano may have told him that Giorgione had many love affairs. Since he promptly and in the same connection states that "he was most estimable in character through the whole course of his life" the reference should not be given any other implications than that he was impressionable, attractive, impetuous and in love with love. Vasari dwells upon his excellence as a player of the lute, which caused him to be frequently invited to parties of distinguished musical people. But it was the art of design which the brilliant boy selected for his profession and for which he was most richly favored by nature. In return for his natural endowment he gave back to nature his whole-hearted consecration as a student of truth. Presumably with Leonardo in mind Vasari remarked that Giorgione was the rival of the great Tuscans in the formulation of a "more modern style for painting."

He succeeded wonderfully both in oils and in fresco, giving mystery to his shadows, a spirited vitality to his figures and "counterfeiting the freshness of living flesh better than any painter anywhere." The most varied manners both of designing and painting a picture were chosen by him, according to the wide range of his interests and his subjects. He was both versatile and resourceful and in painting many Madonnas in Venice and portraits which, much to our surprise, were called "life-like," he gave to these old themes a renewed freshness. It is possible that Vasari had been told the portraits had the same *existence* which makes even his fantasy seem real. I can hardly believe that he ever cared much about realistic illusion or what we call a "likeness." His conceptions and compositions were, we can safely assume, more original than his execution although he experimented with different methods and sometimes unsuccessfully. Fresco evidently appealed to him.

He had seen frescoed house fronts in Castelfranco and Bassano and may have helped as an apprentice on such jobs before he left his birthplace. His first fresco in Venice was his own facade at S. Silvestro. Ridolfi, who saw what survived of this work in the 17th century, described "ovals containing musicians and poets, also fantasies in chiaroscuro." He painted the entire facade of the Soranzo Palace with representations of fanciful stories. We learn of a landscape of Spring in fresco which was beginning to crumble even in Vasari's time, in other words, during what should have been the painter's own life had he not died so young. For the Fondaco dei Tedeschi, the warehouse of the German merchants in Venice near the Rialto Bridge, he was commissioned in 1507 to paint the walls facing the Grand Canal. This was a proof that he was already famous for the

site was the best in all Venice. Vasari says he was given complete freedom to invent and imagine whatever he pleased and his caprice was well known and well liked. The life-sized figures were "faithful to nature but not imitative" and "represented no individuals either ancient or modern." The biographer, in admitting that he could not make them out, added that he could not find anyone else who could explain them to him. Faithful to nature, yet too fantastic to illustrate or to portray with any specific clarity, the paradoxical Giorgione was consistent to his own ideal of lyric truth.

The wall of the warehouse facing the Rialto was subsequently painted by Titian. Vasari states that this opportunity came to the pupil through the intervention of that same gentleman of the Barberigo family whose portrait he described as having been painted by Titian but exactly in Giorgione's manner. I agree with Blashfield and Hopkins who, in their translation, added a footnote which reads, "the whole commission for painting the two sides of the Fondaco was probably given to Giorgione but he shared it with his pupil Titian, perhaps by Barberigo's wishes but more probably by his own." Lodovico Dolce[1] claimed that Titian was so successful with his symbol of Justice over a doorway that Giorgione's friends told him he had never done better and that this made the teacher jealous in the thought his pupil had surpassed him and led to an estrangement. Since the bulk of Titian's work from 1508 to 1512 was derivative from and tribute-bearing to his friend and leader, and since we know (both from Vasari and Michiel) that he was Giorgione's executor and the heir to his studio, the story of a quarrel between the two men is now considered

only malicious gossip emanating from Dolce and others of Titian's idolatrous admirers who were anxious to exalt their hero at his leader's expense.

The question as to whether Titian was the same age as Giorgione or twelve years younger is one in which I agree with the opinion of Herbert Cook, whose reasoned and well-documented argument can be found in the appendix to his book on Giorgione[2] and with Hourticq[3] whose chapter in La Jeunesse de Titien, on the date of his birth is worth reading. The majority of writers take the aged Titian's own word for it, as contained in a begging letter to King Philip II of Spain claiming that he was ninety-five (not eighty-three) in 1571 and, therefore, born in 1476-7. I am amazed at this faith in the unreliable memory of an old man who was proud of his longevity yet concerned about it too and conscious of payments overdue from his royal patrons. If we still accept 1477 as the date of his birth then the first thirty-three years of his life are a total blank so far as all records go. Since Titian's name does not appear on any of the papers relating to the Fondaco commission and the payments for its execution nor indeed in any old letters, or documents earlier than December, 1511, and then only on a receipt for payment at the completion of the frescoes in Padua, it seems safe to say that in 1507 he was an unknown studio assistant on that inconspicuous wall of the Fondaco facing the narrow street. His paintings were invisible from below and could only be seen from

[1]Lodovico Dolce "Dialogo dell Pittura" 1557, intitolato "L'Aretino."

[2]Cook, Herbert—Giorgione (Bell & Sons, London 1907) Appendix II, p.123.

[3]Hourticq, Louis, La Jeunesse de Titien, Paris 1919.

SELF PORTRAIT AS DAVID   BRUNSWICK

Copy of a lost GIORGIONE

*A fragment of the David with the Head of Goliath re-
ferred to by Vasari*

Engraved Head of GIORGIONE
by HOLLER, *18th Century*

the upper windows of houses opposite. Confirm-
ation of our inference that he was probably ex-
ecuting his master's designs is to be found in the
18th century engravings by Zanetti of the frescoed figures.[1] The ones given to Titian are in the
same style as those attributed to Giorgione with
the exception of the rather Teutonic allegory of
Justice and of a single realistic young man which
is very typical of his early drawings. But the most
convincing evidence is Vasari's statement that
Titian was only eighteen years old in 1507 when
he admired Giorgione's new manner of painting
and imitated it. It is unlikely that Titian would
have allowed that to go uncorrected in Vasari's
second edition if it had not been literally true.

Vasari refers to many works by Giorgione
which we do not recognize from his comments.
Some of them suggest a tendency of the painter
to technical bravura and the overcoming of self-
imposed obstacles. What was said about one of
his pictures has always whetted the desire for discovery. The head and shoulders of a young man
"his breast covered with armour" which represented *David With the Head of Goliath* and was
in the words of Vasari "a portrait of the master
himself according to common report" seems to
describe the original from which the damaged
fragment of a stern young warrior's head and
shoulders now in Brunswick, would appear to be
a 17th century copy. The mouth in the surviving
picture turns down at one corner in the expression

[1]Zanetti, Anton Maria "Della pittura veneziana e della
opere publiche de veneziani maestri" Venezia MDCCLXXI.

of a moment's emotion as in the engraved head for the title page of Vasari's book and in Holler's print of the 18th century. Both were based on the original David to which the biographer referred.

In the first edition of his Lives, Vasari attributed to Giorgione the small altar painting of *Christ and His Cross*, which worked miracles at S. Rocco, and was a great shrine. In the 2d edition, without altering the former information, credit was given to Titian. He added, however, that many people considered it the work of Giorgione. I have always suspected that Titian may have told Vasari that he did something to it long after his master's death. The earlier and more dependable source of our knowledge, Marcantonio Michiel, indirectly refers to the S. Rocco *Christ* as an apparently well-known work by Giorgione.[1] Of course, it is not on his Lists. Like the *Madonna* of Castelfranco it was painted for a church altar. Michiel was making an inventory only of the easel pictures privately owned in Venice.

The crux of Vasari essential to my purpose may be condensed as follows: "About the year 1507 Giorgione, not content with the manner of painting practiced by the Bellini, began to give to his works an unprecedented softness and relief" which, as we learn from his other comments, was achieved by the use of either cool or warm, transparent or impenetrable shadows, as the particular subject might require. Having seen this novel, resourceful technic of Giorgione's, Titian, "being at that time but eighteen years of age," left Gian Bellino for Giorgione and painted numerous works in fresco and also some portraits in which he followed his leader very closely. "Giorgione had a reputation of being a willing and careful teacher of whatever he knew." Such generosity was not true of Titian. Paris Bordone, one of his few apprentices and pupils, lamented that Giorgione, who had never spared himself for others, was dead.[2]

"While Giorgione was labouring to his own honour and that of his country he was also much sought after socially and he delighted his many friends with his admirable talents as a musician. At this time he fell in love with a lady who returned his affection. She became ill of the plague and, visiting her, he too became a victim and so violently that in an incredibly short time he passed to another life. This happened in 1510, in his 34th year—to the grief of his many friends to whom he was dear for his affectionate nature and to the infinite loss of the world bereft of his genius. But the world and his friends were the better able to endure his passing because *he left behind him* two pupils who were excellent painters—Sebastiano of Venice, later Friar of the Piombi in Rome, and Titian, who not only equalled him but was even destined to excel him."

Now, the deductions which I need to stress from Vasari's references, are the following: (1) Giorgione was an inspiring pathfinder and, like all other animating leaders of a new school, experimental to a fault. (2) He painted, presumably on commissions, many madonnas and vital portraits, infusing a new spirit into old forms. (3) He was considered the best of all painters of flesh tones, not even Titian excepted. And this reputation was probably based chiefly on paintings of the nude. (4) He liked to paint in fresco

[1] For the exact reference by Michiel I refer the student to the Italian text of Michiel at top of page 291 of Lionello Venturi's Giorgione E-IL Giorgionismo.

[2] For this anecdote about Paris Bordone, see Vasari's Life of Titian.

and was given many opportunities. The Fondaco dei Tedeschi commission reveals his enormous prestige as early as 1507. The fantasy of his figures was enjoyed even while it was incomprehensible. (5) About that time he had changed his style and adopted an arbitrary light and shade to both soften and accentuate the modelling of his forms. He either enveloped heads or figures in a colorful space or else they emerged brilliantly out of a deliberately dense penumbra. The eighteen year old Titian became his imitative follower and assistant. There were rumors that he had become a rival with the murals and the portraits. (6) Giorgione was self-effacing and untiring as a teacher. (7) Some of his subjects seem to have been chosen less for their expressive possibilities than as opportunities to reveal to his pupils how technical obstacles could be overcome. He experimented and demonstrated and this was especially true of his later years. (8) The world was comforted when he died by the knowledge that his work would be carried on by his pupils. In 1510 Sebastiano and Titian were no longer merely studio assistants, but able and well-known young men. They are spoken of as "left behind him" as if their relation to the master had been almost as close as that of sons or heirs. This disposes of the theory that there was unfriendly rivalry and of the legend that Giorgione was jealous of Titian. In the Life of Sebastiano we learn from Vasari that he was called to Rome in 1510 to paint lunettes for the Farnesina Palace and that he never returned to Venice but became a colleague of the Florentine masters and a close associate at first of Raphael but later and for a longer period of Michelangelo. After Giorgione's death he would have had only a month or two in Venice to carry on his Venetian leader's unfinished starts. That was Titian's task and privilege.

Now, let us turn to the earlier and, as a rule, the more reliable authority, Marcantonio Michiel. He was a connoisseur and collector who, between 1525-45 visited all the Venetian collections of contemporary painting and made lists of what he had seen. The owners could have purchased their pictures directly from the artist's studios and so the attributions at this early date can be trusted. The cultivated man who compiled these Lists may have been something of an expert. But whether he was or not he would have exposed an agent's deception since he knew all about the painters, their methods and their associations. Scholars have accepted his word as conclusive. The list of Giorgiones privately owned in Venice during the twenty years of Michiel's visits to collectors can be found in the appendix where I have added comments on possible identification of a few paintings not yet generally acknowledged. Only four of the Giorgiones to which Michiel referred can be recognized today with complete confidence that they are originals —the *Thunder Storm with Soldier and Gypsy*, known in Venice as the *Tempesta*, the *Three Philosophers*, or as I think it should be called, *The Three Wise Men*, now in Vienna, the *Sleeping Venus* of Dresden and, incidentally mentioned, the *Christ and His Cross*, in San Rocco, Venice.

From Michiel's lists we learn that Giorgione's art was evidently in great demand shortly after his death. This is shown not only by the number of original works in private collections but by the fact that even copies were sold. Three of these copies were thought important enough to be cited by this connoisseur, which indicates that they were not student work but commissioned replicas or variants executed either by the master's assistants under his own supervision or by respectful colleagues. We learn further that two out of the three paintings credited to Giorgione which we can surely identify today were acknowledged by their owners at the end of the first quarter of the sixteenth century to have been finished by his pupils who, mentioned by name, turn out to be the same men Vasari had spoken of as his surviving partners, Sebastiano del Piombo and Titian. We are told by Michiel that Sebastiano finished the *Three Wise Men* and that Titian added a landscape and a cupid to the *Sleeping Venus*. The Cupid which Michiel saw is no longer on the surface of the great picture in Dresden but, when the canvas is examined as I have seen it against a strong daylight, the contours of the cherub are clear under the murky repainting. And the X-ray has located and outlined the exact position of this little figure which Titian probably supplied after his leader's death as a popularizing embellishment.

The X-ray has also revealed evidence of great historical importance concerning the date of the *Three Wise Men*, for the plates disclose that the drawing of the distant landscape, the figures dressed in oriental costumes, and their underpainting in the technic of the Fourteen Nineties, indicate the original influence over this picture not only of Bellini but of Vittore Carpaccio. Since the accurate Michiel states that the work was finished by Sebastiano and since the heavy grandeur and academic formalism of the Magi as we see them today are very like his saints in the

churches of S. Bartolomeo di Rialto and S. Giovanni Crisostomo in Venice, it is safe to say that we have an illustration of this pupil's special privilege of practicing the new manner on his master's unfinished earlier projects—a carrying forward with sixteenth century chiaroscuro of his leader's Bellinesque beginnings. Rich in the adolescent Giorgione's compositional invention and lyrical conception *The Three Wise Men* only needed a more suave modelling and a more sophisticated elegance of execution to become a saleable product of the new, modernized academy. The foreground with its low, flat shelves of rock and its little stones might almost have been painted by Giovanni Bellini himself, and as early as 1488. The picture still carries an atmosphere of the Quattrocento. Long before I heard about the findings of the Roentgen rays and before I knew Dr. Wilde's surprising opinion from the plates that Giorgione's own stylistic and technical development over a number of years can be seen on this one canvas, [1] I had often ventured the thought in conversations that the young Giorgione himself stopped work on the picture and that, although it was begun as a phase of his first period of Old and New Testament romanticism (and the foreground and the great dark rock at the left are relics of that earlier period) it ended with the best and most grandiose technical performance of which his pupil Sebastiano was capable in 1510 before he left Venice for Rome.

Louis Hourticq[2] stubbornly refuses to believe that Giorgione was ever anything but a Quattro-

[1] Rontgenanfnahmen der Drei Philosophen, et seg.—Johannes Wilde Jarbuch 1932, pp. 141-52

[2] Le Problème de Giorgione by Louis Hourticq, Librairie Hachette 1930.

centist thus disdaining Vasari's statement that his last period was very different from his first. Since the *Three Wise Men* was carried on by a pupil then, argues the Frenchman, it must have been an unfinished work of his last year, a sample of what he was doing when he died. It must mark the farthest limits of his development. It is impossible, therefore, that he could have painted the *Sleeping Venus* in Dresden, which cannot be the work which Michiel saw in the house of Jeronimo Marcello. So runs the Hourticq argument. Michiel is made the court of last resort to determine the character of Giorgione's art and yet the one painting cited in his journal which confirms Vasari as to the artist's swift progress in mid-career, namely, the *Sleeping Venus* of Dresden, is challenged as a witness in spite of the fact that the picture exactly corresponds to the description and that even Titian's Cupid has positively been discovered under a smudge of repaint. Hourticq cannot admit this fact for it ruins his case. There is no conflict at all between the testimony of Michiel and that of Vasari. Michiel was listing only collectors' pictures and they were chiefly early works for the excellent reason that the middle period from 1505 to 1508 was largely given over to fresco and the last period just before he died was inclined toward the experimental, resulting in unfinished things which became the responsibility of the junior partner, Titian, to do with as he pleased. The works not completely achieved by the master's own hand were naturally in less demand because, soon or late, they were partially Titianized. The *Sleeping Venus* however was purchased by J. Marcello in spite of such collaboration which the owner must have frankly acknowledged. There was

another picture on Michiel's list, an undiscovered *Dead Christ on the Tomb*, which was described as "retouched by Titian."

In the commentary of Vasari one derives the impression that he was much more interested in Giorgione's later developments than in his earlier works. Hourticq claims that the biographer attributed to the teacher a few High Renaissance characteristics he had encountered in his pupils who no doubt had given their leader credit for setting their feet upon the path of progress and who were assured that he would have painted more and more as they were doing if he had not been interrupted by death. It is an ingenious theory based on the fact that Vasari was an intimate of Sebastiano and that he himself really knew Giorgione only from his reputation. In my opinion what Vasari learned about Giorgione from Sebastiano was true and understated, a perhaps grudging tribute of acknowledgment for liberal influence and guidance. Vasari confirms Michiel about the collaborations with Sebastiano and Titian which explains the prominence achieved so promptly by these gifted young pupils. Giorgione's role in Venice was obviously very much like that of Leonardo in Florence and Milan. That he was "a willing and careful teacher of whatever he knew" and that he "left behind him" two prominent assistants who were able to carry on his important work, these sentences have more weight in supporting Vasari's comparison of the Venetian leader with Leonardo than any resemblance of the two pathfinders in their modelling with light and shadow. There was a Leonardesque restlessness in the man Giorgione after 1507. Apparently he was indifferent to finishing compositions once invented or to following through with the less personal conceptions after they had been composed in out-line and underpainted. In a period dominated by the subjective nonconformity and inventive daring of such men as Leonardo and Michelangelo it was natural that Vasari, the art editor, should have stressed that accepted phase of Giorgione's career and character which made the best news—which was making history. It was news indeed that a new leader in Venice had arisen who was so iconoclastic as to break with the Byzantine tradi-tions both for ecclesiastical subjects and for im-posed design, a new pathfinder so conscious of his mission to establish precedents of inventive independence in Venice that he staked no claims to credit for canvases of his studio which his partners could carry on and sign with their own names for all he cared. Paul Cézanne, abandon-ing his canvases in the fields near Aix, or allow-ing his boy to punch holes in them or his servants to use them as fuel for the fire, is only a more striking modern instance of the same age-old creative attitude.

The "Thunderstorm at Castelfranco" As the One Autograph Giorgione

Chapter Three of The Leadership of Giorgione

AN old painting must meet three requirements to be regarded everywhere as a perfect autograph of its artist. First, its authenticity must be proved beyond dispute by a genuine signature, or, if that is lacking, by contemporary records which are in themselves unquestionable. The second requisite is that the picture must retain something, at least, of its first texture and surface. No matter how skillful the restoration and scholarly its conjecture as to the original aspect of the workmanship the handwriting of the artist's own brush work must be legible, as it can never be if it has been covered with repaint. Of course, if time has done its worst and the painting is a mere relic of itself it cannot be autograph. Yet I prefer to peer through a tragic dimness like that of the *Christ* at S. Rocco to catch, perhaps, a glint of the artist's own handling than to see a reconstruction which may or may not be as the artist intended. Even a con-

temporary's careful retouching, which has left the handwriting of design unchanged will, nevertheless, conceal the handwriting of brushwork and make a picture less than autographic. The third necessity is that the autograph picture must have been integral and undivided at its origin. Hand and mind must be one. There can be no intrusion upon what Bernhard Berenson calls the "artistic personality" of the creator and his essential purpose and expression. This rules out studio collaborations on works conceived and designed by the master but executed at least in part by assistants or apprentices.

It is difficult enough to find autograph works by any of the masters of the Italian Renaissance. We have Mr. Berenson's clear statement in the Preface to his Lists that "hand and mind were seldom one" in the pictures of that period, when collaboration was taken for granted and when "no important work was undertaken without assistants." The difficulty becomes extreme in a case like that of Giorgione who died at thirty-three and probably signed none of his works.[1] His whole career as an independent creative artist is contained within a span of ten years, from 1500 to 1510, and more than half of his working time must have been spent on frescoes which have vanished and, perhaps, on supervising the work of his pupils. His experimental methods in oil led, no doubt, to the darkening of the shadows, as in the *Knight of Malta*, and even to general deterioration and this, in turn, to early retouching by his own associates and followers. We have seen that he worked in the closest partnership with two pupils who were his friends, and very able painters they were, one of them a great technician almost from the outset. It was this greatly gifted junior partner, Titian of Cadore, who took to himself, after his leader's death, some of the unfinished things which interested him, carried them on or repaired them. In at least one instance he completely repainted the sadly damaged surface of one of his leader's madonnas, making the picture his own, with his square brushstroke and his sharper outlines. I refer to the *Gypsy Madonna*, now one of the great treasures of Vienna. Under that canvas the X-ray has discovered the same oval face with pensive eyes and the same generalized Christ Child we know so well in the famous Giorgione at Castelfranco. And it is necessary here to stress with repetition the fact that Michiel's records, while giving their documentary authentication to the *Three Wise Men* and the *Sleeping Venus* as works which were conceived and designed by Giorgione, lists them explicitly and with emphasis as partly from the hands of Sebastiano and Titian.

The only other paintings referred to by Michiel as works by Giorgione are the *Thunder Storm with Soldier and Gypsy* and the *Christ Carrying His Cross* of San Rocco, Venice. This last work fails to meet the requirements of an autograph work because Michiel's reference is challenged by Vasari's contradictory attributions in the same book (his second edition) to both Giorgione and Titian and because the picture, though very beautiful, is a ruin. Of course, there is one famous painting which might well be considered autographic even without mention by the earlier manuscripts, so unquestioned is the hypothetical evidence. However, the tranquil *meditation* for a memorial chapel altar which is the glory of his native town of Castelfranco, a picture considered by Ruskin one of the greatest in the world, has been so often and in parts so badly repainted that, for me at least, it has now only a little more paint quality than a good color print.

There remains but one picture which survives the test of being pure, unadulterated Giorgione, the *Tempesta* of the Academia in Venice, that "*Thunderstorm at Castelfranco*," scene of his childhood memories, wherein are to be found the unique fantasy of his whimsical imagination and his rare genius for closely knit pattern. Fortunately this little landscape with figures can be the firm foundation for our further study of the man, the perfect equivalent of himself which can and should aid us in our search for just such a person in other less autographic works. It meets all the requirements. It is documented as by Giorgione, without mention of a studio assistant or a posthumous collaborator. And, God be praised, it is

[1]Unless the mysterious V V on the *Young Man* in Berlin and the *Brocardo* in Budapest stand for Zor Zi.

THUNDERSTORM AT CASTELFRANCO   VENICE

GIORGIONE

in excellent condition! Let us then study the *Tempesta* as an autograph of the master, remembering, however, that although it contains the promise of greater things to come it is still an early work.

A summer storm with ominous thunder clouds cleft with forked lightning advances upon a sultry, shadowy woodland where, near a rushing blue rivulet, a young mother nurses her baby while a young man stands on guard. Here, we feel, is the inspired recall of some intimate emotional experience. The eyes of these young people are averted not only from each other but from the threatening sky. Some acute situation is at a moment of crisis. The exciting weather has affected their thoughts and emotions but they are so much agitated from within that it is almost a relief to sense the surrounding turbulence. Even the weird illumination of the town, "their familiar world grown strange to them for a moment," and even the strange green of the leaves and the sudden darkness in the woods and the lightning flash in the blue-black distance and the walls of Castelfranco suddenly gleaming out of the murky air fails to distract those two from an unsolved problem. It is their own story which the sky dramatizes. With its coming rush of wind and rain that sky is at the center of consciousness not only of the young man and the young mother but of all of us caught up by the emotion of the picture. The pyramidal design, with active storm in nature at the apex and passive storm in humanity at the base, is significant of Giorgione's mystical mentality. Landscape has come into its own in occidental art. Here we have for the first time a landscape with figures instead of a figure composition arranged against a landscape backdrop.

But the elements of this painting are so mixed that it is difficult to classify it. The observation of a condition of light at a particular moment of time anticipates impressionism. The choice of a dramatic moment with a story untold but suggested anticipates XIXth century romanticism. And this dreamlike apparitional fantasy of a nude woman nursing her child in wild weather and the strange details like the twin columns, meaning we know not what, all the incongruous imagery sets up in the beholder what is analogous to, although probably innocent of, our ultra modern XXth century preoccupation with the subconscious as it has recently permeated pictorial art. However, the most modern characteristic of the picture is its geometrical and functional design, its almost abstract relations of contrasted and repeated lines and shapes. The tense moment depicted includes controlled as well as uncontrolled elements and the conflict of storm and calm finds its equivalent in the pattern. Out of colorful darkness accents of white leap to the eye from left to right and back to the zig-zag of the lightning. Inverted planes bisect the space diagonally and so dynamically. There are also nervously active angles, exhilarating semicircles and stabilizing verticals. It was Giorgione's genius to play upon the emotional potentialities of both lines and colors. These expressive functional details we shall find consummated in the *Pastoral Music* of the Louvre. The palette of the *Tempesta*, crimson, acid-green, moss-green, bright blue, a flashing silvery white and a deep blue-black make up a chord of resonant intensity. The texture, too, is one of spontaneous felicity. Flowers, ferns and rivulets are delicately drawn into the subdued richness of the tone. Very sensitive is the anxious face of the little mother. Debonair is the grace of the youth with the pilgrim staff and the nonchalant stance, an attitude in which chivalry and indifference, detachment and devotion, seem to be curiously mingled. Who that has ever seen this picture in a good light, can fail to carry away a conception of the artist and the man Giorgione as he was in his first maturity, at a time of inner stress, before he had come through some introspective maladjustments to an art of wise and glowing philosophical commentary on the outer world?

The compact design and the ambiguous poetry of Giorgione's autograph picture should be compared with an autograph work of Titian's at a corresponding age and stage of development. We should choose for the comparison one of the occasional canvases Titian painted during the last years of Giorgione's life but not under his influence, prophesying instead the unfolding of his own career as he was to pursue it vigorously and into an impressive old age after he had emerged from the spell of his leader's influence. This spell was much stronger during the first few years after Giorgione's death than in the years preceding that event. There is a picture in Antwerp, begun before 1510 though finished perhaps long afterwards, showing Cardinal Pesaro recommended to St. Peter by the abominable Pontiff Alexander Borgia. In its deferential tribute to the Church as an institution it reveals the youthful artist already a diplomat and it reminds us of his incessant seeking of favors from the Hapsburgs even in his later days of greatest prosperity. Compare its backdrop of Baffo's ships on their way to war with the Turks and in need of St. Peter's protection on the high seas with Giorgione's moody

lyric on interesting states of mind or even with the serene mountain valleys of Giovanni Bellini in which the light of late evening or early morning ministers to a life contemplative and, to that extent at least, relates to the religious subject. As for Giorgione's organic relationships between figures and their setting, there is no trace in Titian's early autograph picture. The only tie that binds is that of specific reference to personages and their possessions.

But since we are inviting comparative attention to the most Titianesque early Titians which correspond in chronology to the one autograph Giorgione, it is only fair that we should select not only a courtly ceremonial painted on a commission but a pastoral which, in Giorgione's own vein, suggests an entirely different character. I am thinking of the popular picture of a countryman and his girl in Bridgewater House, London. The cool Palmesque tonality of this painting indicates that it may have been done as late as 1514, which would be about eleven years after the *Tempesta* by Giorgione. And yet I believe that both artists were of approximately the same age when they painted their two self-revealing love lyrics. Titian's *Allegory* is an unimaginative pictorial embodiment of the trite but ever-popular theme of the Three Ages of Man. Whenever he turned to a pastoral Titian's style was countrified rather than idyllic. The substance of this charming picture in London is simply the sharp awareness of the swift flight of time and the sound advice to lovers to make the most of their moments. He was not given to introspection nor to such whimsical imaginings as love in a tempest. Enough for him the imagery that is never outworn and that everyone understands; chubby babies and the decrepi-

THREE AGES OF MAN   BRIDGEWATER HOUSE, LONDON

Two early examples of Titian's own self expression. Even in the pastoral which derives from Giorgione in subject, the design is less functional and the meaning more explicit.

POPE ALEXANDER RECOMMENDS CARDINAL PESARO TO ST. PETER   ANTWERP

TITIAN

tude of the very old as foils to the amorous dalliance of a bronzed shepherd and his blonde sweetheart. As Mather wrote "she looks up into his face with adoration and unreserved desire. Nothing could be more explicit." The landscape background is a portrait of a place—realistic like the people portrayed and inconsequential as an aid to the design or to the expression. The old man contemplates a skull on a hillside of the middle distance which is otherwise of no importance to the picture. Even in the far lovelier *Advice of Venus* in Rome, better known as *Sacred and Profane Love*, the young Titian revealed himself as an impersonal materialist and a masterful young artist, exulting in a glorious world he had observed closely and in the exercise of his extraordinary powers as a realistic and decorative painter. He was a man from whom life was to withhold nothing, who was to see it clearly and whose skillful hand would always perform as his cultivated mind directed. His figures, singly or in groups, could be lifted out of their setting and enjoyed as specimens of brilliant objective painting. They contributed to an allegory or to a story or to a decorative frieze like the popular picture in Rome, in striking contrast to Giorgione's figures which contributed notably to a complex design or to a dominant mood but which were too self-contained (meditative is usually the word) and too absorbingly interesting as individuals to play roles in a pictorial drama. Details also of Titian's landscapes were delightful in themselves but independent of the picture as a whole whereas Giorgione's landscapes existed with a life of their own which required a coordinated use of every line and mass. Giorgione, unlike Titian, was seldom stately in

his compositions nor facile and brilliant in his execution, nor comprehensive and normal in his range of interests, nor well adjusted to and a part of the world he lived in. On the other hand, he was more sensitive, more inventive, and more subtle in the intellectual and emotional refinements and, after 1508, he came into a more accommodating attitude without relinquishing any of his special qualities. Everything was integrated, interdependent and unobtrusively stylized. And everything continued to evoke moods. All the parts functioned from first to last in orchestrated symphonies of emotional design.

In the *Tempesta* of his youth and the *Pastoral Music* of his full maturity, although the created moods are antithetical, there is an identical kind of lyric enchantment, a similar genius for evoking with incongruously assembled figures, nude and clothed, the otherwise inexpressible music of a state of mind. Titian's autograph *Allegory* with the amorous shepherds is only a trite story and a portrait group of models posed in a particular place. It is a plain-spoken picture in which there is no mystery and no ecstasy. Much later, in London's glorious *Bacchus and Ariadne*, Titian would achieve on his own account a marvelously unified and intense emotion. But, at the period when the *Pastoral Music* of the Louvre was painted, he was only a decorative and realistic painter, the best of his kind but not yet a profoundly expressive artist. In his autograph creation, the *Thunder Storm*, Giorgione revealed a mind unlike any other in the history of art, such a mind as could make landscape the instrument for subtle and varied rhythms. Artists from his day to our own would emulate his expressionism of design but never surpass it. If we know the young poet-painter who both conceived and executed the autograph *Tempesta* we can hardly fail to find the same man grown older in the pattern of other works and to see traces of the same hand grown bolder in parts, at least, of pictures not completely his.

The First Period,

1494 - 1504

Chapter Four of

The Leadership of Giorgione

THE combination in the same picture of functional structure and an intense, slightly disturbing strangeness is the rare distinction of the one sure Giorgione, the *Thunderstorm* at Castelfranco. It will be found in all the best paintings of later masters, such as Tintoretto and El Greco, but it is less characteristic of our lyrical founder of abstract pictorial romanticism. Perhaps the fact that the combination is so clear in the *Tempesta*, his autograph for all of us, may account for the hesitation of the critics in attributing to Giorgione pictures which lack either one or the other of these qualities. His other really great works possess, it is true, both architectonic and poignantly emotive elements but, after the *Tempesta*, only three times did the artist achieve a fine balance of intellectual second thought with imaginative suggestion and, in the *Venus* and the two *Concerts* to which I refer, there is no element of suspense. If there is an enigma in the *Pastoral Music* it does not matter. Whenever the reasoned pattern in his serious pictures was a delight for the mind, then the expression was that of a concept or of a contemplative but not of a nerve-troubled mood. In the less important creations however of his first period, when the impetuous fantasy stirs the emotions with a baffling vagueness the design is more truly expressionistic invention than organic construction.

There are in Padua two long narrow panels of landscapes with little figures which once decorated wedding chests and which, in the catalogue of the art gallery there, claim Giorgione's authorship. The designs are alive with functional rhythms and the moods are sharply emotional. It must be admitted that the emotions are extravagant and lacking in his exquisite reserve and this may be due to the fact that the actual execution was by another hand and at a later period. To anyone who believes that Giorgione never painted dramatic action, that he did not even set the scene for a drama with appropriately exciting effects of lights and darks, the notion that he ever drew the more poignant one of these two cassones in Padua is roughly rejected. Yet, for me the thought is neither unreasonable nor unwelcome. The after-sunset glow, the black trees silhouetted against it, the mysterious gloom between the edges of the forest and the sky, contain the strangeness and intensity which are in the *Tempesta*. The excited actions of the little people in the foreground seem an emanation from a light in which anything might happen. Agitated figures move wildly through a haunted light, enacting a strange story or a dreamlike mixture of stories, including the death of Adonis. The figurines are crudely drawn and poorly painted. Clearly they are the work of a copyist. And yet they move as if to strange and intense music, the vibrations of which linger in our memory. "Emotion remembered in tranquility"—that was Wordsworth's definition of the lyric and it was, I believe, Giorgione's central conception of his art. Stormy emotions can give pleasure in retrospect no less than the serene ones, especially to a subjective artist. The two almost unknown furniture panels, which the special student of the Giorgione problem should not miss when he stops at Padua to see the frescoes of Titian, are pervaded by an insistence upon the abstract in emotional design which relates them to the influence of Giorgione if not to the master's own mentality. They were done after he died. In fact they have a modern appearance. One would almost say that Arthur B. Davies had done them when he was very young, or some earlier 19th century romanticist enamoured of the

Giorgionesque idyll. That, of course, is an exaggeration but I use it deliberately to show Giorgione's modernity. Mr. Berenson's attribution of the actual paintings to Romanino is probably correct and I see his hand in the gay companion piece to the scene of violence at nightfall. No matter what the story of that other and happier panel the impression is that of a country dance on a richly wooded estate. The same eery half-light serves now a different purpose making the swing of the dark tree tops as lively against the bright sky as the romping arms and legs and flying ribbons of the golden boys and girls playing together in the dusk. My guess is that Romanino was commissioned to paint these cassones but was asked to follow the patterns of a pair of furniture panels by Giorgione himself which we have not discovered. Perhaps they had gone to pieces even at that time and, instead of repairing them, the owner ordered copies made on a larger scale. Assuming that the execution of the copies gives a misleading impression as to the original brushwork of the originals I venture to attribute the designs, at least, to Giorgio's studio.

In his boyhood Giorgione must have been richly endowed with the instincts of play and make-believe which are the beginnings of the creative urge. His playfulness was never outgrown. It is enriched with universal symbolism yet still the motif of the great *Pastoral* of 1510 and important then in any study of his art. He could touch lightly on the emotions of recognition and surprise and was glad to oblige the great world with philosophical and aesthetic sublimations of the earthly passions, or of materialism in general when it is ill at ease with itself. In this he was the forerunner of Watteau and also of a single phase of the many-minded Shakespeare.

Max Eastman says that the first law of humour is that "things can only be funny when we are in fun." Giorgione knew that the visible world which is the one concern of the painter is only made intensely interesting to others when one has been intensely interested and that it only seems really lovable when one is truly in love with living. To be in fun, to be in love, to be at play and to be at rest were often best to relieve the storm and stress of life. Comic relief was wisely employed by Shakespeare for his tragedies. Also he knew the value of pastoral interludes and passages of word-music which ease the hurts of the mind. In his quintessential lyrical phase he resembled Giorgione as he recalled Titian in his objective range and impersonal power and especially in the plays abounding with spectacle and action. But the songs, so lilting and so merry, "with a hey and a ho and a hey nonino," were fraught with a hint of melancholy and the pastoral "As You Like It" is a parable of universal wisdom. From the start Giorgione had alternating moods of grave and gay, of melancholy and serenity. Like Shakespeare he could take off on a flight of fancy only to return to reality with a half-brooding, half-quizzical nonchalance and a shy, contemplative sympathy for human grief.

The first period culminated in a few great pictorial conceptions which gave fresh meaning to traditional subjects; the journey of three wise men in quest of something greater than science; the faith of the simple-hearted in the birth of a Saviour and in the growing light of a new day for the world; the electric storms which whirl and crash yet alter only the moment and even tend to calm the inner agitations; the wistful thoughts of motherhood, and about motherhood as an ideal; the incredible memory of a horror that is past when the sun is high and the breeze smells sweet. The same period had begun with decorative trifles and these persisted with no less significance than the more serious expressions. They show, even through ruin, restoration, or the work of copyists, not only his handwriting of design but his real delight in graceful and irresponsible pictorial diversion. The allegorical poesies were frankly meant to please and not to be taken seriously, and yet they are almost complete in character. They bear the same relation to the *Christ and His Cross* at S. Rocco and to the Pitti *Concert* as the songs in the "Forest of Arden" to the author of Hamlet.

Giorgio was once a country boy of marked talent and he must have had a rich and powerful patron, probably Caterina Cornaro, whose portrait we know he painted. She it may have been who sent him to Venice for the best possible training in his art. His imagination and his early acquaintance with the Greek myths and the Latin poets would have qualified him for designing those decorative panels for wedding chests, screens and lockers which were already the fashion and for which, no doubt, he created a greater demand. Ridolfi wrote that he was one of many furniture painters working in the crowded quarter near the Rialto when he first lived in Venice and helped Bellini in his busy shop. To find the earliest of his exercises in applied art, the first poesies which, from internal evidence if not from documents, suggest Giorgione in his teens, has been the ambition of every student of the subject.

A clue is sometimes discovered which has significance. In Michiel's Journal for 1525, there is mention of a very early work by Giorgione entitled *The Birth of Paris* which belonged to Taddeo Contarini. Thus we know that in his first period and probably in adolescence he was interested in the unfamiliar tale of how Paris as a baby had been exposed to die because Cassandra had been moved to prophesy that he would destroy Illium. Two shepherds had come along, so ran the tale, and discovering the child's plight, had rescued him to fulfill his fate. The moment of their discovery of the baby in the mountains was the incident the boy Giorgio thought appropriate for pictures. There is a copy by Teniers and also an engraving of a lost painting on this theme which once belonged to the Archduke Leopold. And, at Budapest, there is the copy of a fragment containing the two shepherds. They stand, one of them pointing a forefinger, as in the engraved picture, in similar though not identical postures. The obvious and disarming childishness of this scrap of evidence makes it unnecessary to apply to it any qualitative standard.

Sir Martin Conway happened upon, and was quick to acquire, two quaint little panels with the shepherds finding the baby Paris and giving him to a nurse. The landscapes contain farms and a tower, the like of which, we are told, are still to be seen in the Valley of the Brenta near Castelfranco. Now, the crudities of juvenilia have done no good to any reputation. Perhaps, with that in mind and because, like Morelli before him, Mr. Berenson is ever ready to defend Giorgione from his imitators, his List does not contain any of the Paris-legend pictures which the great critic leaves in the pleasant realm of "let's suppose." Since not one of them shows any of Bellini's qualities it is a fair inference that they

are but folk painting from the Alpine foothills. Yet if we enjoy believing with Lord Conway that Giorgio painted them himself, somewhere near Bassano, then the idea is not in the least impossible.[1]

The earliest works of Giorgio which reveal the influence of Bellini[2] and hint at his own budding talent are the two decorative landscapes with figures which hang in the Uffizi in Florence, one on each side of Bellini's *Allegory of the Tree*. Tradition is insistent that all three belonged together in the Villa Medici at Poggia a Caiano and it is clear that the older master in his most capricious fantasy and his best pupil, promptly taking fire from it to launch himself as a fanciful decorator, are revealed side by side in one of their epoch-making relationships.

In 1490, or perhaps a little earlier, Bellini read a Mediaeval French poem entitled "Le Pelerinage de l'Ame" which set him thinking aesthetically. It was a devotional poem and the pictorial vision it inspired was devotional too but it permitted imaginative invention. The humour is probably unintentional. The scene is a marble-paved platform in Paradise overlooking a river bordered with caves. The babies playing around a tree are infant souls. An open gate is guarded by Saints Peter and Paul. The Madonna is seated under a ruby-red canopy idly watching, though in an at-

[1]Professor F. J. Mather owns a small furniture panel with a naked baby on a hillside at nightfall which seems to represent Paris before the shepherds rescued him. It is of later date and shows more expressive skill than the Conway panels and may be attributed to a follower of Giorgione, perhaps Dosso Dossi.

[2]The *Christ and His Cross* of the Gardner Museum in Boston is a copy of a lost Bellini, possibly by Giorgione. Philip Hendy has attributed the student-copy to Palma.

titude of prayer. The old poem had done strange things to the holy people. A children's party seems to be attended by saints, the ones Bellini had been commissioned to put into his next pictures. The background of his dream was a river with grottoes, very striking, with its golden lights and dark shadows of late afternoon. Sebastian and Job were bored looking at the children from the end of the platform opposite the Blessed Virgin. Sebastian was also sad. He had received no sympathy for his martyrdom with the arrows. There were too many other saints at the party. The Christ Child had left his Mother's arms to play with the other babies. It was all then, very obviously, a dream.

The newcomer in the studio, young Giorgione, conceived rich possibilities for adapting and extending the incongruous dream fantasy in which his revered master had indulged himself. Instead of sacred personages he would take Venetians of high rank, place them in the gardens of their country villas, let them enact some romantic old fables. They would really have nothing more to do than to supply bright colors and vertical lines to landscapes already decorated with the arched loggias of distant architecture. They would be in oriental dress. Their pale, oval faces would catch the light. An armed knight wearing a plumed helmet, a king enthroned, lake water reflecting the sky, dark cypresses and sheep pastures, farms and castles, all would lead the eye back to high mountains. Trying to give a better idea of Giorgione's early subjects than could be conveyed by the titles Ridolfi described them thus: "In the shadow of pleasant trees men and women stood about happily enjoying the tranquil air." We think of Pater's "listening to time as it flies." Ridolfi's

description of a scene of tranquil indolence all but authenticates the Uffizi pictures although it is true that both panels pretend to depict trials and judgments, and may have been, as Mather suggests, decorations for court room lockers. Only the landscapes, however, and the figures around the throne in the *Fire Ordeal of Moses* are worthy of even the boy Giorgione. The stiff little puppets in the foreground of the *Judgment of Solomon* were surely the work of a clumsy fellow-pupil. Carpaccio has influenced these figures far more than Bellini and it is he we think of in the National Gallery's little idyll, No. 1173, which Berenson calls "close to Giorgione." Certainly the high bluff at the left balanced by the figures at the right is prophetically Giorgionesque. It is a charming school piece in which wild animals are at large in a pretty park and a kind philosopher-king in a sylvan nook receives the tributes of his subjects while all is well with a dewy, innocent world. The immediate influence of both Carpaccio and Giorgione is unmistakeable in this picture which I would date a year or two earlier, rather than later than 1500.

While still in Bellini's studio Giorgione, no doubt, had attracted attention and won patrons for his furniture paintings with romantic subjects from the Bible. This must have led to commissions which kept him busy during the first few years as an independent artist. It was then, I believe, that he started the underpainting of the *Three Wise Men*, now in Vienna. The X-ray plates made for Dr. J. Wilde have revealed that the oldest of the magi, in the underpainting, wore a bizarre oriental headdress with a diadem over a loose cap. It was, of course, tentative, a mere experimental indication of an alternative silhou-

GIORGIONE'S THREE WISE MEN   VIENNA

Copy by TENIERS

This shows the original dimensions

ette. The face was flat and formless. Seen in profile, his white beard tilted upward, the patriarch gazed at the sky. We are vaguely reminded of Carpaccio. Giorgio must have sketched this figure not long after he left Bellini. Unsatisfied or uncertain about it, he must have gone on to the other figures since they appear to have been carried further. The seated youth, his gaze also upturned and his head in profile, appears in the plates very much as we see him today—modelled with care and yet brushed more freely than in

Sebastiano's over-painting and with a characteristic glimmer in the high lights similar to the whites of the *Tempesta*. I suggest that Giorgio was taking his time with the figures, finishing with his own hand only the first plane and its slabs and little stones; also the great dark cave at the left. Much of that was cut away later than the 17th century, since we know the far finer and ampler original design from Teniers' copy for the Archduke Leopold. The pyramidal composition with the figures at one end, the great rock at the other and the distant landscape at the apex created both a retreat for the mind and an outlet for the eye to the sky and the hills. "The whole effect" as Mather writes in his Venetian Painters, "is to make of the screened and shadowy foreground a spiritual sanctuary." Giorgione had found a theme in the Bible which gave him a chance to contemplate the intellectual detachment of three scholars united only in feeling and purpose. All of his men and women, singly or together, were destined to wait, to meditate, to pursue their separate thoughts and to cultivate their idleness. That he lost interest in this picture after he had placed the three men in a subtle relation to the landscape and established their individual characters, and that he then probably instructed Sebastiano as to desirable changes in the directions of the heads and the folds of the robes which would make for a more unified and balanced rhythm and that finally he entrusted to him the actual over painting of the figures and the sylvan distance, must be clear to anyone who has studied the cold, grand manner of that able painter in his Venetian youth. Instead of the sparkle and surprise of the *Tempesta* and its wealth of temperament all seems frozen with a grandiose formality and the colors, even in what should have been an ecstatic sky of dawn, are unemotional.

Sebastiano was not in the studio in the earliest years of Giorgione's independent achievement but he was probably one of Bellini's best pupils in 1504 and I have a notion that his services were borrowed when an able assistant was required. There had been collaboration on the jobs of the Bellini bottega and there continued to be collaboration on the commissions which came to Giorgio's own establishment. The years 1500 to 1504 must have been crowded ones for the young chief of a progressive movement who had graduated with much prestige from Bellini's school so that he was immediately successful. It is certain that he had more to do than he could manage without assistants. Those who believe that Titian was born in 1476, or a few years later, are sure that he and Giorgio formed their partnership immediately after the time when they had been fellow pupils of Bellini. Before I can believe that I must see something to explain why Titian was not heard of before 1508 when, according to Dolce, who was close to Titian and knew whereof he wrote, Giorgione gave to the youth from Cadore his first chance in employing him as an assistant for the Fondaco frescoes. It was called a great opportunity "for one not yet twenty years old." It is of course possible that he came to his new leader as early as 1504 when he was sixteen if Dolce and Vassari are to be trusted. If that were so I could well believe that he painted portraits in Giorgione's style and under his direction and perhaps helped him with the earlier frescoes which led up to the Fondaco commission. In spite of Mr. Berenson's daring and stimulating conjecture I cannot see Titian as the author of Lord Allendale's beautiful and important *Adoration of the Shepherds*.

Even less is he recognizable to my eyes in the earlier and smaller pictures of the same group of works, the *Holy Family*, formerly in the Benson Collection, London, now owned by Lord Duveen, and the National Gallery's little *Adoration of the Magi*. Certainly there were assistants who executed the major part of these pictures from Giorgione's designs, but in my opinion the boy Titian could not have been one of them. The more super-

Detail of HOLY FAMILY *from Adoration of Shepherds*   LORD ALLENDALE, LONDON

GIORGIONE AND ASSISTANT C 1503

The design of the entire painting as of the two paintings opposite was by the master, but the execution must have been by an unknown assistant of Bellini who was borrowed when needed

HOLY FAMILY   LORD DUVEEN

Studio of GIORGIONE 1500-1

ADORATION OF THE MAGI   NATIONAL GALLERY, LONDON

Studio of GIORGIONE 1500-1

ficial reason for attributing the really great Allendale *Adoration* to the same artist and at the same date as the little pictures I have mentioned with it is the recognition of the same models, especially for the blonde Madonna with her hair drawn back over a high prominent forehead. Berenson saw the difference in execution and for a long time he assigned the two lesser works to Catena while stating that the important *Nativity* was by another hand.[1] The more profound kinship between the three pictures is their possession in common of Giorgione's genius for filling a space with a variety and a fine balance of design-elements in new and attractive arrangements. The recurrence of the same models is only of interest in referring the execution of the three pictures to a closely affiliated studio. It might have been the shop of Bellini about 1504-5, for the Joseph of the little Epiphany is the Peter of the S. Zaccaria *Madonna* and the old, white bearded Saint Jerome, so splendidly painted in that great altar painting, has the pinched features of the Joseph in the Allendale and Benson Holy Families. The old man occurs again, however, as the grandest of the *Three Magi* in Vienna which, as we know, is a documented collaboration and which I think Giorgione worked on for a number of years before his pupil Sebastiano finished it about 1508. The favorite models of Bellini, during the first decade of the sixteenth century, were shared apparently by the master with Giorgione and with his later pupils Sebastiano and Titian.

The designs and their idiosyncrasies which we find in the so-called Allendale group of pictures are, to me, conclusive as to their compositional invention by Giorgione himself between 1500 and 1504. Curiously enough the execution re-

vealed is different in each work. Lionello Venturi saw Giovanni Bellini in the draperies and G. M. Richter saw Sebastiano in the cold, dry landscape of the Benson-Duveen *Holy Family*[2] but Richter does not fail to see that only Giorgione could have planned the curvilinear pattern of the picture and the compact placement of the family as a unit at the center, with an arched opening into space at one end and a closed wall, rich with tactile sensations, at the other. My own guess is that the young leader designed and perhaps even underpainted all three of these pictures and then lost interest in the execution of any other part than the landscape of the large *Nativity*. The little *Adoration of the Magi*, the *Holy Family*, and the group at the cave in the Allendale *Adoration of the Shepherds* were, I believe, painted by an unidentified pupil of Bellini, who was eager to help Giorgione whenever called upon.

The *Epiphany* in the National Gallery is charged with the restrained animation of an imagined halt when the three Orientals and their retinue arrived at the stable in Bethlehem. The tribute of the Magi is received with dignity in contrast to the stir and crowding of horses and men. The effect of glowing lantern light with night shadows is romantic and imaginative and there is a rhythmical disposition of the forms in space. One could almost believe that Giorgione both designed and executed this little picture himself but the colors are not characteristic.

The splendid landscape of Lord Allendale's large *Adoration of the Shepherds*, in London, is not only the master's own in conception but ex-

[1]Venetian Paintings in America, p. 256, footnote.
[2]Unfinished Pictures by Giorgione, by G. M. Richter, Art Bulletin, September, 1934.

Detail of ST. JEROME

S. ZACCARIA, VENICE

BELLINI

Detail of THE OLDEST PHILOSOPHER

from THE THREE WISE MEN, VIENNA

GIORGIONE & SEBASTIANO

aware of something precious that was worth keeping even as a wreck, something that has vanished now perhaps beyond recall.

Far more important, even if no documentary proof ever turns up, is the *Judith* in the Hermitage, Leningrad, which, at the Italian Exhibition in Paris in 1935, was acclaimed by all the authorities as an indisputable Giorgione and an important work entirely by his own hand. It has the overtones and evokes the afterthoughts which proclaim the master himself and which the imitators of his subjects and his technic were powerless to achieve. In its technic the date of the picture appears to be as early as 1504. As we shall see, this *Judith* leads directly to the *Sleeping Venus* in Dresden and to the monumental figures of women for the Fondaco frescoes. It is thus a link between the periods. The style remains somewhat Bellinesque but the expression is more like Leonardo with just a hint of Raphael, to whom it was once attributed, and more than a hint of 19th century romanticism. It is a culmination of the series of early works dealing with the pathos of a remembered tragedy in the serene and spacious sunlight of another day. The actuality of her violent deed is hard to believe for the daintily feminine Jewish heroine in the pearly freshness of a morning light when all the world seems clean and new. Recalling the horror, but only as one not wholly reassured on waking from a terrible dream, she touches her sword with shrinking finger tips and looks down upon the tyrant's severed head helplessly and blindly. Beyond the stout trunk of a tree the air is filled with a golden glow, as of the sun rising with the exultation of all who are happy and free. And yet it shines also as only the sun can shine when those conscious of tragic experience are aware of being unable to share in its generously expansive gifts of life and radiance. The significant thing to note about this painting is the use of a legendary subject as a mere pretext for the subjective expression of a familiar emotion. In Mantegna's powerful little picture of *Judith in the Tent of Holofernes* (Widener Collection) we see an example of the illustrative approach to the pictorial depiction of the theme. Though sculptural and synthetic it remains a narrative. Giorgione always employed the particular as a vehicle for suggesting the universal and this he apprehended through a conception or a mood intimately personal.

Of the *Madonna* at Castelfranco it is possible to say that it is most interesting as the outstanding example of Giorgione's occasional willingness to do the conventional thing and to pay the appropriate tribute with at least an air of impersonal dignity. It is not the last of his Madonnas if I am right about the lovely mother and child in a fertile mountain valley which is known to us only through a copy by Cariani at Bergamo. Perhaps it is not even the last Madonna attended by Saints if, as I incline to believe, it was Giorgione and not Titian who painted for a private chapel the unfinished *Madonna with Francis and Roch* at the Prado, Madrid. And yet, this famous memorial for his home town's parish church was a respectful farewell to the past as he turned his face to the future, a last gesture of affection to Castelfranco and the generous knightly patrons there, to the good Bellini and his gravity, his sweet and noble seriousness, his love of material textures, finally, to the church as an institution, to its saints as symbols and to all the old standardized images. In this composition the traditional monumentality is so much in evidence that one hardly notices the innovations. Consequently, these discreet changes had all the more influence, and the painting, so deferential to the old order, was a formative factor in the future advances towards a new freedom of Bellini and his followers. The different levels of the shaft, near the top of which sits the Madonna, are enriched with contrasts of texture, color and form. The arms of the Constanza family in a round yellow medallion and the green and violet brocade which hangs from the base of the throne reveal Giorgione's decorative use of detail in a larger and more functional way than such details had been used by his predecessors. Inverted perspective leading our gaze upward and outward into space is achieved by the simple expedient of S. Liberale's lance and its long, autographic diagonal. Above the high crimson screen, which is the background for the two standing Saints, one looks out over a silvery expanse of early morning sunlight. The distance is expressed chiefly by values of increasingly pallid colors although the arrangement of trees and buildings in a diagonal recession aids in the illusion of deep space. What might be two disconnected landscapes dividing the interest is avoided by the integration of the whole picture in one pervasive, tranquil light. The picture is personal in spite of its desire to be formal. Several writers have been tempted to remark that the Virgin looks wistfully absent-minded, and to suggest that she is not dreaming of her Divine Child nor of the Kingdom of Heaven. The two defenders of the Faith, the man of action and the cloistered man of prayer and peace, are together yet alone with their thoughts. They seem united only in a common loyalty and reverence.

I regret to add that every time I have seen the *Madonna* of Castelfranco it has moved me less. The last restoration has been the worst of all. It seems now inferior in every way to Bellini's *Madonna* in S. Zaccaria painted the following year. In composition it is less unified than the grand old man's *Madonna* of 1510 at the Brera in Milan, where the shadowy mountain landscape ascends to a central height behind the throne, sloping grandly to right and left without need of the buttressing Saints. In color it has less quality. In expression it is less really religious. Bellini, who made his Madonnas his central and most cherished purpose, could be realistic with his particular models for sacred personages and with his specific places for landscape backgrounds without ever losing any of his devout homage or any of the fervour of his pious prayer. Giorgione took the beauty of goodness in his stride along with the goodness of beauty, but when he symbolized the worship of sanctity it was with reverence but not with intimacy and ardour. It was for him a universal ideal but never quite a personal reality. He loved his *Christ* of S. Rocco because although he was sublime like a God he also suffered like a man. The *Madonna* of Castelfranco is worshipped but not as the Queen of Heaven at all—nor even as the Blessed Virgin. She is just the universal mother of a son who may grow up to be a man of war or peace. She is just the woman one happens to love and to need. It would have been natural and right for him to give to his Madonna the features of his own beloved. There is a traditional belief that he did.

Giorgione and His Pupils

Chapter Five of
The Leadership of Giorgione

FROM 1505 to 1508 much of Giorgione's time was consumed with his exposed and doomed fresco paintings. Even if those frescoes had decorated the interiors instead of the exteriors of Venetian buildings it is doubtful whether their duration would have been much longer. Yet even if the painter had been told that his work could not endure would he not have persisted in such work? It was, we know, a quality of his character to be quixotic in whatever he undertook and to regard explorations, with the odds against him, as more important than a consistent record of success in already well cultivated fields. This pioneer instinct in the man was overstimulated by the wealth of new ideas in general circulation. What had not been done he would do. What had been done badly he could improve upon or demonstrate that it was not worth doing. All the while his exacting taste and intensely personal mind required of him that he

paint a few pictures containing the essence of his philosophy. All the cassones and romantic abstractions and even the merely decorative frescoes were only preparatory to a few great pictures which, I like to think, he had already conceived. The first of his big themes was to be the Sleep of Woman, the second the Loneliness of Art, the third Art and Nature. Better known titles which are household words, identify today the results of such plans. There were two distinct men in the man Giorgione. One was impetuous, intrepid, iconoclastic and capricious, adventuring for the sake of experiment. The other was a profound artist whose mind sought outlets not in allegories from the Middle Ages nor in mythology from the ancient Greeks but in personal symbols of ageless and universal truth. The culmination of the crowded years of his first maturity, 1505-08, was not the spectacular success of the Fondaco frescoes but the exquisite start he made on one of his master works, the *Sleeping Venus*. As we know, he never finished it with his own hand. What we see today is a blend of the best of Giorgione and the best of the young Titian but both marred by scars of modern retouching. The same two men were destined to be mingled again on the other masterpieces *The Concert* of the Pitti and to a lesser extent on the *Pastoral Music* of the Louvre.

The *Sleeping Venus* might well have been on its way by 1507 but the Fondaco commission interrupted. The masterpiece could wait. It would be all the better for his technical experience in painting many large draped and nude figures. Hellenic ideals at this time dominated his thought; ideals for balancing and tranquilizing flesh and spirit, body and mind. Yet in many ways he was unlike the old Greeks and he did not attempt to be a good and consistent pagan. By honest conviction he was a humanist and a builder but in many of his moods he preferred to be a playful poet and when he was most himself he was a mystic. The monumental, the lyrical, and the mystical are to be found, all three, in his best pictures. There are less than ten of them. If we could be sure that he received permanent credit for these great works, most of which he did not live to finish, then all the rest of his production would not matter very much. Yet we need to know the lesser things. If I give to them his name it is because I think that they were done under his immediate influence and instruction. The imitators of Giorgione who painted from a greater distance were mere followers of a fashion in art. But the master himself may have planned the work that was accomplished in his studio. As for the grand manner which he adopted during the period of

the frescoes it was, we believe, alien to him and yet perhaps a very necessary exercise of his own inherent capacities for grandeur, a quality to be found in the *Madonna* of Castelfranco and her male champions and no less in the *Judith* left alone with her deed.

That full length *Judith* of 1504 may have been the first real response of Giorgione not only to the general awareness of a classical inheritance which was soon to launch the High Renaissance in Venice but also to his own latent powers as a self-effacing constructive decorator. There had been shy intimations of this consciousness of the Greeks in a few of his earlier works. That now ruined cassone, the *Apollo and Daphne* in the Seminario, Venice, was a frieze of little figures moving blithely on one plane, their fluttering garments making a linear melody. But for the *Judith* he had composed on a vertical plan with variations of straight and undulating lines. He contrasted the static and inert tree and sword with the very feminine curves of the standing woman's slender body, and the marbled smoothness of her skin with the sparkle and crinkle of her draperies and the gleam of her jewels. A rich variety of texture was always one of the means of Giorgione's expression but never the end, never the true essence of it. The essence of the artist in the *Judith* is found in the serene and glowing ambience and the free and vast distance. The structure of the figure itself is subordinated to a sense of surrounding space. His primary interest for that picture was in the suggestion of the individual, no matter how prominently placed, subconsciously affected by the larger life of nature, by that outer world which is indifferent to the shocks of personal experience. And yet something appears on this upright canvas that is new in his art, something which indulges the eye with what can be called the architectonic gratification. The influence of Raphael's mind had travelled northward and brought to the leaders of painting in Venice the more anthropomorphic conception of life and the more sculptural and space-filling function of line. For a while both Giorgione and his young disciple Titian were impressed. They assimilated profitable elements in their environment which were making for a Venetian branch to the School of Athens. Giorgio could receive as well as give and learn as well as teach. He took fire from art as from life. The boy Titian only derived his culture at second-hand from Giorgione, at least until six years after his leader's death. But, at the outset, during the time the teacher was trying to bring out the individuality of his pupils by encouraging them to show their real bent, Titian's trend in a fresco was towards a robust and colorful realism while the ever experimenting Giorgione seems to have tried for a time to discipline his own romantic approach in order to make his forms larger and more monumental. He had decided that for a year or two he would renounce his patterning in depths of idyllic landscape and modify his plan of light and shade so that it might accord with wall decoration and a suggestion of low relief. The mat surface of fresco could absorb the most brilliant pigments. The antique world could come to life on the facades of Venetian palaces.

In an earlier chapter we noted that he began with the front of his own house. Ridolfi had seen "in the rise of the chimneys groups in chiaroscuro" and, probably between the windows, "ovals containing poets and musicians." The success of the experiment led to commissions for similar decorations on the fronts of other palatial buildings. All these frescoes disappeared centuries ago. Most of the delectable colors were mottled and faded even in Ridolfi's day. We have only Zanetti's weak engravings to give us any clue as to what a few of the frescoed figures attempted to do in line. In the prints two of the standing women are, for Giorgione, surprisingly majestic and impersonal. Seated figures of a woman and a man do show the expected angularities and intimacies of pose as of persons caught off guard and unconscious of being seen. The fragmentary survivals of round girlish heads, shoulders, arms and knees, anticipate Tintoretto's *Graces* in the Doges Palace. The best of these on the German warehouse were attributed in the old picture book to Titian and this must have meant that they were from his wall on the side street. And yet I know that they were done from Giorgione's designs for they are precisely in the same style as his large nudes which faced the Grand Canal. The Allegory of Justice however was Titian's work and there is no doubt at all that he drew, and on his own initiative, the stocky youth who held a dagger behind his back. Whether the assistance to Giorgione on the Fondaco was Titian's first public appearance after his school days with Bellini is problematical. Giorgione's helper on the Soranzo Palace and the other pre-Fondaco jobs was someone other than Titian, probably Morto da Feltre who, according to Vasari, had studied Greco-Roman fresco and mosaic. The few still Bellinesque or early Giorgionesque easel pictures, chiefly on religious subjects and quite crude, which have been attributed to the boy Titian by contemporary critics from internal evidence, are

Figure in fresco from the Fondaco dei Tedeschi ascribed to TITIAN
Engraved by Zanetti

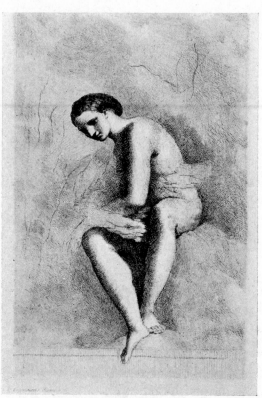

Figure in fresco from the Fondaco dei
Tedeschi ascribed to TITIAN
Engraved by Zanetti

Figure in fresco from the Fondaco dei Tedeschi
ascribed to GIORGIONE
Engraved by Zanetti

It is noteworthy that the boy Titian was theatrical in the allegory of Justice and the young man with
a dagger while Giorgione was intimate in his seated figure of a girl

logically dated 1506-7. During the last two years of Giorgione's life Titian painted derivative portraits close to his teacher yet more objective and clever; also he started a few pretentious things like the *Pope and Cardinal Before Peter* in which he was more independently himself.

Giorgione's Portraits had come into great demand by 1505. He needed time to do so many other things! Persistent were the calls for his unconventional Madonnas and Biblical romances. But how could he paint all these smaller works and also fresco house fronts? So much to start and so little time to finish anything! There was that first masterpiece at least to plan and put on canvas. He needed the help of gifted and intelligent young men who had special ability for portraiture and for the composition and drawing of assembled figures. Fortunately in the famous school of Giovanni Bellini there were two such pupils. Giorgione needed those lads, Sebastiano and Titian, as much as they needed him. The matter was easily arranged.

Sebastiano was attracted to Giorgione because he too was a humanist and musical. What he had done in Bellini's studio has never been discovered although there is a school piece in the Academia in Venice which has one figure strikingly like his favorite type of Venetian beauty, the dark heavy eyebrows, the broad face and frame, the small faultless features. Giorgione at once set him to work on the *Three Wise Men*. For a while he must have revised the picture himself with his pupil's help. But it is my guess that after 1505 he turned it over to Sebastiano, supervising his repainting both of the figures and the landscape. I am one of the few who think that

it would have been a better picture if he had left it in its original state, as a primitive example of his own art. But Sebastiano could only learn a picture-form and only gain a stylistic sense through practice and he was very promising material. Soon he was able to execute from his teacher's indications the handsome altar painting of S. John Chrysostom, showing the old man enthroned off center, seen against a background of columns, the attendant Saints and womanly Virtues standing on a lower level to right and left. The color is rich yet reserved, suggesting that Giorgione had seen to that. Sebastiano was given to exaggerated tactile sensations and tonalities. The *Salome* in London for instance is smooth and cold and the *Madonna with Sebastian and Other Saints* in the Louvre is heavily painted and the colors are unpleasantly hot. Yet the same man is clearly apparent in both. There is grandeur in his decorations for *S. Bartolomeo* di Rialto. I mention these vertical panels of 1507 because, in their dignity and their illusions of air and space around the male saints standing in Bellinesque niches, they show the goal Giorgione already had in mind for Sebastiano when he renounced his own *Three Wise Men* that his assistant might find himself in its execution.

From 1505 to 1510 a chronological review of the works of Giorgione requires an almost equally close attention to the step by step development of Titian who was destined to be his junior partner and a collaborator on his unfinished masterpieces. He had come to Venice from his mountain home at Cadore when he was a child of ten to learn about mosaic from the Zuccatis. His first teacher of painting was Gentile Bellini but Vasari tells us that he felt himself a misfit in that illustrator's studio and was soon transferred to the larger school and the more tolerant rule of Giovanni, the wise and kindly high priest of the painter's art in Venice. Those writers who cling to the belief that Titian and Giorgio were born the same year are compelled to make it appear that Titian was very slow in showing talent since, at their computation, he was an unknown assistant to Giorgione as late as 1508 at the age of thirty-one, with nothing to his credit in the way of acknowledged previous achievement. Berenson has tried to find what would be slavishly Giorgionesque pictures, almost copies, which he might have done between 1500 and 1507. I remember on his Titian list the ruined *Soldier and Young Mother* of Compton Wynyates which he evidently regarded as an imitation of the *Tempesta* and the *Eros* or *Boy with Arrows* in Vienna which he supposed to be a variant or commissioned copy of the leader's *Shepherd Boy with Flute*. He has included important works as well, Lord Allendale's *Adoration of the Shepherds*, Mr. Goldman's *Bearded Man with Hand on Book*, *La Schiavona* now owned by Herbert Cook, and the *Gentleman of the Barberigo Family* in the National Gallery. Of these pictures only the last two are on my list of early Titians and I hold that they were executed not earlier than 1509 by Titian as a precocious youth of twenty-one instead of as a retarded man of thirty-three who was still imitating his classmate. In his new book on Venetian Painters Mather sees the hand of Titian in the mountain background of Bellini's *Baptism of Christ* in Vicenza painted in 1501! But if he had been able to paint so well at the turn of the century why was there such a falling off in his works during the seven years which were

to elapse before the Fondaco frescoes when we know he was only an assistant, and during the eleven years before our first surviving evidence of his genius which is documented with a business paper—namely the frescoes at Padua? Suida, Hourticq and Longhi, critics with whom I disagree as to Titian's greatness by 1510, are in my opinion entirely correct in attributing to his hand before 1508 only such works as are similar and inferior to the Fondaco figures. These writers and also G. M. Richter are convinced he was born about 1488 or -89. They have discovered juvenile works, some of which are also on the list of Mr. Berenson. He of course dates them earlier.

The first Titian must be the one which Richter came upon in an Italian private collection—a madonna with the infant John. The Virgin is enthroned against a curtain in a stereotyped Bellini convention but already the picture reveals Titian's typical baby and fat little boy and his blue sky and white clouds. It is a curious blend of the old master's standardized specialty and the young pupil's budding talents for opulent decoration which would result many years later in the colorful *Madonna of the Cherries*. A *Jesus Blessing* in the German Protestant church of Venice was brought to light by Suida as a very early example of Titian just emerging from his childhood influences and from his boyhood training. It shows a trace of the Byzantine which at the outset he had seen in mosaics. There is something too of Durer who had loomed large at Cadore and there is even more of his lifelong conception of a dignified and stately Christ. The style of course is clearly "School of Bellini." The hand is held palm upward as in "the earliest Madonna" which Richter found. Suida had dis-

CHRIST BLESSING   CHURCH OF HOLY APOSTLES, VENICE

TITIAN

Attributed by Suida to the school days of Titian

MADONNA WITH INFANT JOHN   PRIVATE COLLECTION, ITALY

TITIAN

The earliest of all Titians, painted while a pupil of Giovanni Bellini

covered a Lucrece so much like the profiles of stout women in the Padua frescoes that a photograph should be enough to convince a skeptic that it is at least a copy of a Titian of the first period. Chronologically it may be later than the *Tobias and the Angel* in S. Caterina, Venice, which Titian told Vasari he painted in 1507.[1] This is confirmed by the resemblance of the angel to the heads of the Fondaco fresco of that year. A pretty lady with outspread wings has taken a stumpy little peasant boy by his hand and they walk in pleasant places. In the old engraving from the picture the landscape is more emphasized.

Between the Fondaco frescoes in Venice and the Scuola del Santo frescoes in Padua there must have been a rapid improvement in Titian's composition of figures in landscape. To the year 1509 I would assign such charming works as the *Madonna with the Infant John* in a flat, flowery landscape, now one of the minor items of the Mellon Collection, the *Nymph Wounded by Cupid* in the Wallace Collection, London, (there is said to be an earlier variant in Italy), and the beautiful *Holy Family* in landscape in the Collection of the Marquis of Bath. The portraits of this time are extraordinarily fine for a man so young. Herbert Cook's important *La Schiavona* was thought to be Caterina Cornaro by Giorgione while it was in the Crespi Collection of Milan. It is signed T. V., the proper initials, since Titian's family name was Vecelli. The Berlin *Young Man* is almost universally accepted as Giorgione's pattern for Titian's early portraits. It is no more closely related to Titian's art than his most direct inspiration. That surely is close enough. Stylistically and quintessentially

it is an autograph Giorgione of 1502 lacking only documentary proof. The handsome boy is like a younger brother of the sleeping Venus with the same perfect oval head, and dark hair parted in the center. There is a ruddy glow under his olive skin and these rich tones are contrasted with the grape bloom of a dull blue background and a quilted garment of lilac, showing bluish shadows. The eyes are mysteriously thoughtful and the tapered finger tips scarcely touch the parapet. It is the Ideal Head for an adolescent day-dreamer, a classic generalization, not a portrait at all. Titian was never interested in such distinctions. He went straight to the sitter and painted what he saw whether it was on display or in reserve. Charles Ricketts in his excellent book on Titian, pointed out that he had a recurrent tendency to paint the upper eyelid of an equal thickness from corner to corner. I have noticed that most of his men and women are round eyed but never with wonder or reverie, only in candour and intelligent polite attention to the spoken word. The eyes he painted are not starry, remote or elusive like the eyes of Giorgione's dreamers or thinkers. Titian's stout Schiavona with her hand on a sculptured ledge which shows her own profile in low relief is pleased with herself and with the world in general. His handsome bearded man in the National Gallery, London, is clearly Vasari's "Gentleman of the Barberigo family." He would have been mistaken for a Giorgione if Titian had not signed it Titianus. Thus Vasari mentioned the similarity of technic between the portraits of the teacher and his pupil. But in that

[1]Vasari wrote that this picture was in S. Marziale but he was mistaken. The Tobias and the Angel in that church is a much later achievement.

portrait in London the signature of Titian is less conclusive than the characterization. As we say it is signed all over with Titian's objective truth. A novel could be written about this alert and able young man of affairs but not a lyric poem as all Giorgione's sitters seem to require. Incidentally the picture, with its evidence that the quilted sleeve was painted much later than the head, is the first canvas which shows Titian's lifelong practice of starting a canvas and then putting it aside with its face to the wall, returning to it at coldly regulated intervals. This was very different from Giorgione's abandonment of his underpainting in the impetuous interest of a new concept or design, possibly never to return to its final execution. Titian's picture in Antwerp of the two ecclesiastics pleading to St. Peter to give victory to their ships may have been begun in belated fulfillment of a vow before 1507 but it was not finished until much later.

Suida must be sure that by 1509 Titian was not only an accomplished painter but a profound psychologist and distinguished designer. Consequently he gives him Mr. Henry Goldman's black bearded man who looks not at us but beyond us out of a corner of a rather owlish eye. His neck is a simplified column, archaic and structural, a clear sign of Giorgione in 1505 not of Titian in 1509. I wish the picture could be more generally known. It is one of the great art treasures of America. The man's clenched fist rests on a book which lies on a ledge wider than the one behind which stands the stout lady of Titian's youth. It is like that other ledge in rising to a higher level at the right but the rise is less abrupt. The broken parapet of the portrait in New York like that in his Judith has functional

purpose in the pattern. Its reflecting surfaces and its angles are repeated in the open window thru which one can look across the Grand Canal to Palaces opposite and to a distant bridge. Amusingly its curve seems to repeat in its arch of light over dark water the prominent arched eyeball of the dark man portrayed. His expression is baffling —perhaps because he himself is baffled. We would like to know what troubles him. In his abstracted gaze we seem to see his determination to be resolute about something which is not yet satisfactorily settled in his own mind. His unseeing stare relates to the clenched fist on the closed book and perhaps even to the distant bridge at the Rialto. Thus a compact functioning of the lines is also contributory in every detail to the portrait's purpose of characterizing more than a man, of standing for a state of mind which the artist has known in himself and as a universally difficult moment of dangerous doubt and abrupt need for decision. That stance of the sitter between a parapet and a wall with a window opening out on a distant view was much admired by Bellini and the followers of his last phase, especially Catena. It also influenced Titian. His portrait of two men, in Berlin, and of an old man, in Copenhagen, are excellent adaptations of this pattern. So is the *Madonna With the Tree Trunk* of the Bache Collection.

There are critics who still credit him with designing the *Gypsy Madonna*. I am one of those who believe it was begun by Giorgione but abandoned when he designed the *Sleeping Venus* which in its turn he was unable to finish because of the great commission for the Fondaco dei Tedeschi. The landscape motif of the squarish mountain with a low building under it was then adopted for the composition of the new masterpiece. Of course I agree with the majority opinion that the buxom gypsy mother of Vienna with her strong lively baby boy is the work of Titian's realistic and forthright mind and of his able hand. We cannot fail to see his rich impasto and his competent, square touch. It is not even the unsatisfactory x-ray plate which makes me think that the underpainting was by Giorgione. Although Giorgionesque in its oval pensiveness of downcast eyes the merely blocked-in face of the Virgin underneath might indicate only an earlier stage of Titian's emergence from the spell of his master. That is the opinion of Dr. Wilde.[1] But the compact integral design—the pyramidal form, the serene gravity, the rhythms of line and the chord of unusual color with cherry-red, olive-green and azure, these æsthetic elements the young Titian of 1508-09 could follow with a disciple's fidelity but scarcely invent. What he added when he overpainted the picture, probably under his leader's supervision, was a heavier texture, more voluminous draperies and that more explicit and objective mind and vision which his facile, obedient brush instinctively obeyed. The underlying silhouette and linear rhythms and the original color scheme may or may not have been preserved. The x-ray shows either that the underpainting was flayed before it was covered or else that it had never gone into details. What I see in the *Madonna* at Vienna today is a collaboration, a pyramidal Giorgione design and a realistic Titian painting. A little picture of the same date, distinguished by a graceful rhythm, this time a charming composition of many figures with a fine balance of diagonals, verticals and ovals, again reveals, after a drastic removal of repaint, Titian-

esque brushstrokes and heavy folds like those in the *Gypsy Madonna*. I refer to the ruined sketch of the *Circumcision* in the Jarvis Collection of the Yale Gallery. I see the Titian of 1509 working in Giorgione's studio perhaps on his plan for an altar painting's predella.

To Giorgione in the pre-Fondaco years, 1505-07, I have now credited: 1, the revision of the *Three Wise Men* and the supervision of its overpainting by Sebastiano; 2, the designing of the altar decoration for S. Giovanni Chrisostomo which Sebastiano executed entirely himself; 3, the frescoes which adorned the fronts of his own house at S. Silvestro and the Soranzo Palace; 4, Mr. Goldman's great *Portrait* of a brooding Venetian and, 5, the original design and now completely transformed underpainting of the *Gypsy Madonna*. What else can we give him for those years of increasing self-knowledge, self-discipline, constructive experiment and full achievement of his maturity?

If it had not been for that experimentalist in Giorgione he could have finished what he began and made at least his masterpieces entirely his own. But he felt he had a mission. He could not fail in his task of breaking ground in new territory which he could stake out for the other painters. It was his pride to set an example of independence and initiative. It was better to fail than to take the easiest way. It was better to be a barometer of the classical culture and creative restlessness of his period than to live within himself as he might have liked to do. He was the animating spirit of the art of his generation and his patrons, friends and pupils were proud of his

[1]Roentgenanfnahmen der Zigeunermedonna in Oesterr. Jahrbuch 1932, p. 141.

new ideas. And so he tried out, as one of his experiments, differential projects for psychological portraits or ideal heads, projects differing one from the others less in the degree of penetration into the hidden depths of character than in the technic, the scale or the lighting.

Each experiment found its admirers and followers. Thus the *Lady* of the Borghese Gallery, standing, it would seem, at a window, with her handkerchief held taut as a signal to someone who looks to her from outside, is so closely the inspiration of Licinio that many critics think it must be his picture. It is more sentimental and story-telling than Giorgione and at the same time more realistic, but in a primitive way which reminds me, the scalloped head dress and all, of the untrained provincial early American portraits. I marvelled many years ago that Morelli and Berenson were so sure about the authenticity of this damaged curiosity and I continued to be skeptical until I saw it again last summer. It was in process of restoration. One eye was to be entirely repainted and meanwhile it had been blotted out. In spite of this handicap the intensity of the gaze in the other eye held me in fascination. The scientific Morelli for once abandoned his science under this pale lady's influence and acknowledged that, from the merely subjective experience of her presence, he was convinced that only Giorgione could have seen her with such insight and intensity of interest. I think nevertheless that the picture in Rome must be only a copy of a lost original and one which may have been changed freely by the copyist according to his own whims.

The *Antonio Brocardo* in Budapest, in the words of Morelli, "appears to be about to confess to us the secret of his life." He may seem more like Pordenone's portrait (in the Herbert Cook Collection) of the man who looks up thoughtfully from his open book, than like Giorgione's ideal heads of dreamers and thinkers. The master himself was neither sentimental nor realistic. What he did was always on the safe side of the borderline between the intimately lyrical and the sentimental and on the frontiers of a realism which he approached respectfully but never crossed. One can detect details in the Borghese and Budapest pictures which are certainly not Giorgione at his best but which should not be overlooked since they reveal curious idiosyncrasies of his own. Giorgione's rounded hands with long thumbs and the long slender feet of his earlier nudes are mannerisms which are characteristic whether we like them or not. Brocardo was begun by Giorgione, or so it seems to me, about 1506 or -07 but left unfinished like so many other works interrupted by the Fondaco frescoes. In its present state I would relate its final execution to such a follower as Licinio or Pordenone some time after Giorgione's death.

If the Borghese lady and the Budapest man were middle period Giorgiones at their origin then they represent the earliest three-quarter length portraits. It was not, however, until 1509 when the *Knight of Malta* must have been painted that this larger scale attained to such perfection that it quite logically became the model for Titian's grandest and noblest creations of the same kind. The dark twilight landscape behind the head of the introspective young man in Budapest is the third background which we have come upon in the authentic Giorgionesque portraits. First there had been the solid, ceramic blue after Bellini's

backgrounds of his Giorgionesque period. All the right half of the canvas in Dresden may have been overworked by Titian. At the time when the cupid was painted out however the restorer covered with muddy tones not only the section where that little figure had played but many other bits here and there. Even the beautiful torso has had its subtle modelling in full light flattened a little by comparatively modern retouching and Giorgione's marvelous line has been diminished in its magic although I doubt if it was ever really an incisive edge. He always sought for a line that would be lost and found. Giorgione in 1507-08 created the inspired design and painted the rock, the dark red cushion, the sparkling white drapery, the Greek head and the long lovely curves of the slender body which, as someone said, seems "poured out" upon the grateful earth to become in sleep a part of its living calm. The small head is not in a correct relation to the lyric length of the body. It is the poetic license, the abstract expression of a Hellenist but of one with what I like to call "modernist" convictions, one who dared to alter radically if need be the actual proportions. The body of the Venus was copied precisely enough by Titian for his own nude in the Uffizi. But what a difference! In contrast to Titian's open eyed wanton, the portrait of a particularized, a conscious and desirous courtesan, Giorgione's slumbering goddess is the embodiment of an ideal. And even the most important line of the composition, the left leg, stretched deliciously to the utmost, while the whole being is supported and relaxed, seems sheer genius compared with Titian's copy of the same line which is merely expressionless realism. Never was Giorgione's art as a painter a more

consummate joy than in the peaceful, perfect head, the mossy, fern-grown bluff, the shadowed crimson cushion and the crumpled white cloth. Even the distant scene beyond the sheltering rock, with the peaceful valley stretching to the sky and the mountains, and the one graceful tree in the middle distance, affords a prophesy of modern landscape painting. But it is in the unity of the figure with the space and the light and the release from time in the blessed interval of sleep that Giorgione's linear magic conveys its deep and tender mysticism. The long, low hills slope gently in harmony with the goddess and her rest, and the sun is not too hot nor the shade too cool for her sake. Again, as in the *Thunderstorm* and the *Nativity*, little flowers are drawn into the dark green turf. Beauty itself is as a flower.

The sense of serene tranquility in the *Sleeping Venus*, of peace on earth, curiously remind us of a very different picture, the culmination of the same artist's first period, his *Madonna of Castelfranco*. Arnaldo Ferriguto[1] called her "Our Lady of Peace." "Constanza," he writes, "had given up arms. War had ceased and though the great Condottiere sorrowed for the death of his soldier son, yet calm had come to the Veneto." The Blessed Mother, young yet prescient for her divine child, grieves with the donor for the mothers of all the sons who must die at the wars. But the surrounding air is sweet. The silvered radiance of early morning is full of promise and of solace for the living. Four years later, at the crest of his second period, the *Venus* of Giorgione is only another symbol of Peace, a symbol of what Mather calls "journey's end" in the

[1]*Attraverso i "misteri" di Giorgione* by Arnaldo Ferriguto, 1933.

search for true love. "Woman and the earth, the two sources of life, are conceived as in complete accord."

The wistfulness of the artist about so sweet yet grand a subject as the *Sleeping Venus* may account for the fact that Giorgione would not hurry its execution when the Fondaco commission came, nor return to it after he had finished the frescoes. Who knows what it was that may have changed his mood so that he waited for the right moment to return? It is the same spirit, different not in kind but in degree, which did not permit Leonardo da Vinci to finish the head of Christ for his *Last Supper*.

The Approaching Consummation
of Giorgione, 1508-9

Chapter Six of
The Leadership of Giorgione

A S GIORGIONE grew to his full maturity and learned through practice how to give to his works as Vasari related "more tone and relief," he determined to symbolize art itself as a ceaseless activity of the human spirit and of its questing or resting ardours. To sublimate earthly love and sensuous loveliness, to interpret the loneliness of the subjective artist and to create a plastic equivalent for art's relation to nature in glad acceptance of all the good things the physical world has to offer, these purposes led him successively to the *Sleeping Venus*, the *Concert* and the *Pastoral Music*. He wished also to continue his series of universal types and these culminated in the *Knight of Malta*. The writers who have seen in Giorgione only the interpreter of his own introspection or only as the poet of stillness and Arcadian reveries have failed to understand the cross currents and complexities underlying his consistent point of view. To find his art, not merely through documents but through understanding of the man who both conceived and executed the autograph *Tempesta*, makes it possible to follow the evolution of his emotional life and to trace his progress from that early expression of his subtle personal moods to his destined goal.

By 1508 Giorgione's pupils had done so well that they were virtually junior partners. The master turned then with greater freedom to new conceptions and experimental designs, knowing, as he did, that his capable associates enabled him to increase his range since they could transcribe with the aid of realism and of skill in story telling. The imposed subjects of his commissions might require their talents. With the help of Titian and Sebastiano, both of them musicians and cultured men, he could make painting richer for the qualities they all admired in the other arts and also more true to itself in the consciousness of the special scope and limits of each medium. He knew that only in the abstract integration of form and substance, the satisfaction of the instrument, the sounding surface, may be found the essential purity of music. And he knew that writing about life must make the meanings themselves valuable and the audible, sensuous language a minor though always an integrated element of fine expression. As a painter, how could he make the best use of the visible world so that his pictorial language would not be limited to sensuous surface or to structural design or to representation of what the eye unaided can see for itself but could be quite simply and naturally a synthesis of pattern, texture and subject and a symbol for meanings inseparable from the forms and colors, and possessing intrinsic not merely referential value and the mould and tone of his own mind in close association with the minds and hands of his young associates? And what better theme for art than the philosophy and passion of art itself?

The old Sacred Conversations of his forerunners were adaptable to his purpose of making painting a criticism of life or a poem in praise of it. He planned differential arrangements of three or more people conversing or silent together in moments of shared experience. Sometimes one state of mind dominated the group but more often there were different points of view which he typified for his reflective observation. The picture mentioned by Vasari of the Florentine "Giovanni Borgherini when he was a boy in Venice with his tutor in the same picture" must be a lost double portrait from which could have been derived as a variant the sadly damaged

Three Ages of the Pitti Palace in Florence. With complete conviction Morelli long ago accepted this work as a Giorgione and today Suida and other critics agree that only he could have conceived and composed what must have been a pattern for the intimate portrait groups which were to follow in his own and many other studios of the period. What we see today shows characteristics of one or two late Bellini scholars, perhaps of those excellent portraitists Lotto and Catena, or as Berenson suggests, "perhaps a phase of the octogenarian Gianbellino himself." Certainly from the picture as a whole the spirit of youth is absent. There is something direct from Giorgione in the drawing and painting of the young boy day-dreaming at his music lesson. We see him in the stray curl under the cap and in the shadowed, downcast eyes. The rich color chord of his clothes reminds us of the two young men seated on the grass in the *Pastoral Music* of the Louvre. But this something of the master's own has been intercepted on its way to posterity. Vasari mentioned only two figures, the Borgherini boy and his tutor. Of course he attempted no complete description. He was interested to hear that Giorgione had painted the childhood of a well known citizen of Florence. The old man may have been left out of Vasari's account just as he was left out of the conversation in the picture. However, the reference ends with the specific remark that "no two heads show better flesh color or finer shadows" which implies of course a double not a triple portrait. It is probable then that the *Three Ages* at the Pitti was, at its inception, a fresh start of Giorgione's instead of the commissioned work which Vasari saw or heard about. It is my notion that, at Giorgione's death, his old teacher Bellini found the canvas in the studio and that it pleased him. A boy was already painted in and there were indications of a middle aged teacher with a pointing finger and an old man looking sadly away. It would have been a good subject for him—the passing of his generation while his own pupils moulded the mind of youth. What we notice today in the *Three Ages* at the Pitti Palace is the pathetic futility of modern retouching in repairing old surfaces. The picture is now a wreck! But we return to it in spite of the fact that it is in ruins. The young boy is a conception worthy of Giorgione himself and more like him than like the old Bellini or Catena. Berenson's "Master of the Pitti Three Ages" is described as "between late Bellini and Giorgione." I think that the picture was begun by the younger and finished by the older master and his associates. The middle aged man resembles Giorgio's standing shepherd of the Allendale *Nativity* but also the kneeling warrior worshipping the infant Christ in Catena's masterpiece in London. The picture could be labeled Studio of Giorgione for I believe that much would be true even if evidence were discovered that most of it was painted in the Studio of Bellini after Giorgione's death.

In the Pitti Palace the *Three Ages* suffers in comparison with the great picture in the same room which reveals the mind of Giorgione at its best. The idea of the *Concert* was the consummation of his brooding on the evanescence of beauty, the inpermanence of music's raptures and the isolation of the soul. In recent years, ever since Morelli startled the world of art with the first suggestion that the *Concert* was painted by Titian, a majority of the experts have been stunned into agreement. A resemblance of the central figure to Titian's *Man with the Glove* in the Louvre and a general recognition of the fact that the head of the musician at the clavichord shows more structural modelling than was Giorgione's practice and that it was painted with a more crisp and modern brushwork than the other heads, has all but convinced me that this head shows the execution of Titian several years after his leader's death. Nevertheless the pyramidal building up of the figure, the emotion expresssed in the face, the vision of creative ecstasy, of inspiration on the wing, of mute and vain appeal for understanding from one musician to another, these revelations of Giorgione's mind cannot be disregarded. The life of action which the painter of the inner life was supposed to have evaded may be said to include the dynamic life of thought. Such a life was his continual preoccupation.

Improvising at the keyboard the young musician's eyes are illumined with radiance. He looks back for understanding of his exaltation and of his unspoken sadness because the palace of music he has built will crumble when the last vibration is still. Has his old friend the musical monk caught his vision? But no. The churchman with the 'cello only stares with a profoundly respectful, frank amazement. As for the youthful singer of the trio he seems too conscious of his plumed hat. He is quite unaware of what has happened. Later perhaps he will sing and with so clear and fresh a voice that his vanity and insignificance will be forgiven. But for the moment he is only a foil to the ardours of art and mind, only an overdressed discordant presence. Time has taken its toll of this picture. A strip of canvas has been added at

MAN WITH GLOVE   LOUVRE, PARIS
TITIAN
Titian finished the musician at the clavichord in the
Pitti Concert as the Louvre portrait testifies

THE CONCERT   PITTI PALACE, FLORENCE
GIORGIONE & TITIAN
Detail of central face

the top. Collaboration has hurt its unity. The realistic modelling and sentimental expression, short of which Giorgione always stopped, became for Titian and Sebastiano a real danger when it was their task to complete what he had started. This musician's backward look which in Giorgione's conception must have been subtlety itself is now spoiled with over elaboration and over emphasis. How much of this was due to his partners is very hard to measure. And yet the picture continues to testify to Giorgione's own inspiration in its pyramidal composition, in its glowing light, in its color chord of orange, black and white, most of all in its poignant interpretation of art on the edge of the infinite, of the moment of vision at the summit, of the return alone. The

attribution of the picture as a whole to either Sebastiano or Titian is to me fantastic. A single characterization for a portrait was within their reach but, in a group, they saw the relations without subtlety and, not even when they were disciples of Giorgione, were they ever really subjective. Never could they have felt a passionate regret for being far away from those most near, that yearning for the continuance of life at its highest which is in the *Concert* and which for centuries has spoken for Giorgione's special genius.

The iconoclastic critic M. Hourticq in his book "Le Probleme de Giorgione" attributes the *Concert* to Sebastiano del Piombo! This gift to an eclectic, and coldly objective painter in his Venetian youth of a profoundly original and subjective work is based on documentary evidence. In Vasari's Life of Fra Sebastian he relates how this artist while still in Venice and a pupil of Giorgione's became the friend of the French composer Verdelot, choir master at San Marco's in Venice and subsequently at San Giovanni in Florence. Vasari tells that "Sebastiano painted many good portraits in Venice, among others that of his friend Verdelotto, with his pupil Uberto a singer in the same picture." We should disregard documents when the picture itself tells a different story. In this case there happen to be resemblances in the head and hands of the musician at the clavichord to Sebastiano's habitual drawing of over prominent eyes looking back and of long fingers with the joints flexed at acute angles. Both mannerisms however were mere imitations of two idiosyncrasies of his master's. Palma also imitated them. It is true that the artist of the *Concert* is described in detail and that Sebastiano's modelling of a face with the use of strongly contrasted light and shade was always more detailed than Titian's. But whoever overpainted the player of the clavichord of the Pitti *Concert* also executed on his own account the *Young Man*, in the Frick Collection, who wears furs and a red cap and possesses a pair of large, languishing eyes. Since that young man is certainly by Titian I feel fairly confident that it was Titian who finally executed the musician's face and at the time he was painting the *Man with the Glove* in the Louvre. But whether, as I think likely, Sebastiano once collaborated on the picture of his musical friends and told Vasari about it and whether Titian finished it after 1512,

these probabilities are of less importance than the essential truth that the Pitti *Concert* is the one most intimate expression of the poignant lyricism of Giorgione, the great genius of improvisation. It should be entered in the catalogue as "by Giorgione and Titian." Sebastiano's possible contribution to the result is merely a reasonable conjecture.

During the same year that he painted the *Concert* Giorgione probably conceived and executed in large part the Altman portrait of the red bearded man who, I feel certain, was not Ariosto. Even as he had left the central head of the masterpiece in Florence unfinished so this head in New York may have remained in a state which justified Titian in retouching it. The same black background of the *Concert* accentuates the glowing flesh tones of an equally sensitive face. The subjective mood again is one of rather melancholy contemplation. But here the theme is not the frustration of an artist but a frail unfortunate gentleman's doubt whether he will not always fail at the difficult business of living. Recent removal of surface restorations has revealed at least a hint of Titian's technic. Yet when I first saw the Portrait, in spite of its bad condition it was eloquent of its maker's psychological solicitude and his exquisite reserve. I agree with Mather that it is close to the poignant Giorgione in the Church of S. Rocco.

Too sensitive to be a stoic the tortured *Christ* of Giorgione is too sure of his mission and of his strength to appeal for the pity of the ages. The Roman soldier and the fanatical Jew represent the world of militarism and dogmatic religion which Christ had to deal with. The individual's ultimate triumph over the mass mind and

CHRIST CARRYING HIS CROSS

GIORGIONE

S. ROCCO, VENICE

its cruelties is suggested. On a sudden impulse the soldier looks the other way and the Jew loosens the rope to peer into the face of his victim in awe of something he has seen there. Never was anything more touchingly rendered in art than the glazed eye and dry lips and yet the unconquerable, undramatic fortitude, the sense only of an unembittered, sorrowful understanding and of an unflinching, blessedly remote endurance. Those who think of Giorgione as a lover, as a lute player and as a painter of earthly enchantments are apt to seize upon Vasari's second printing in

which Titian was given credit for this picture. But the young Titian who painted the Borgia Pope before Peter and the explicit, over colored *Tribute Money* in Dresden was unable to conceive of spiritual subtleties. He saw everything without bias, handsomely but with a neutral indifference. How could he have imagined a moment when the basest of men was almost deflected from his course by a flash of insight into his victim's soul? Although the painting in S. Rocco is dim today from incense smoke and pious over cleaning, veiled to a mere film of faded tone, yet

TRIBUTE MONEY   DRESDEN

TITIAN

*This is Titian's Christ and its difference from the
Christ at S. Rocco is profound*

the depth and grandeur remain. Curiously the
eyes and brows remind me of the head of the
earth woman in the *Pastoral Music*. Illustrations
of the two details in Elie Faure's "Renaissance
Art," pp. 188-9, will remove any doubts that
whoever painted one had painted also the other.
But the expression is what matters. An overwhelming appeal goes out from this ruined
masterpiece as we feel its inspired reserves of
impassioned idealism and sternly controlled
emotion. There is an inextinguishable intensity
in the gray panel. The accidents of time and
change seem only to have sharpened the meaning.

The executioner is reduced to a greenish blue underpainting in contrast with the rich texture and
spontaneously brushed head and figure of the
Christ. Simplified to its spiritual essentials by its
return to its beginning something in the composition of the three half lengths and in its generalization of a world-shaking truth makes us think
of Daumier, and not only of the Daumier of the
small two and three figure arrangements on one
plane but of the unfinished masterpiece in Essen
on a similar theme, the *Christ Mocked*, one of the
grandest sketches ever painted. Giorgione's *Christ*
in Venice is not a sketch but an abandoned, un-
restored wreck, yet the results are the same. The
colorist and the subtle analyst of character tri-
umphs at S. Rocco over an apparent negation of
color and over the havoc wrought by time and
change. There is an old tradition that the picture
worked miracles. Certainly its modern appearance and its emotional power today are nothing
less than miraculous.

After 1509 either Titian or Sebastiano or both
of them seem to have had access to if not actually
a hand in almost everything Giorgione undertook. The tendency nowadays among the critics
when they find one or the other of the junior partners in something that had been considered Giorgione's in design is to change the attribution from
leader to follower without any explanation to
the student, and without any acknowledgment
that such pictures are Giorgione underneath and
Titian or Sebastiano on the surface; Giorgione in
the conception and the composition, but his followers in the execution, the alterations of detail,
the technical finalities such as scumbling and
glazing, the more advanced passages of realistic
modelling, and the later Renaissance costumes.

Detail: KNIGHT OF MALTA UFFIZI, FLORENCE

GIORGIONE

PORTRAIT OF A MAN MUNICH

TITIAN

Giorgione's generalized symbol for an idea should be compared with Titian's faithful but ennobling portrait of a particular person

There has been a lamentable and strangely deliberate indifference to the unquestionable fact of Venetian collaboration. "In the Renaissance no considerable work was undertaken without assistants." Every painting left unfinished at an artist's death was freely available to his followers to do with as they pleased. Now visitors to museums and occasional students of the story of painting who consult catalogues and text books and believe in the attributions there given are entitled to know that the assistant's helping hand before the master's death and his finishing touches afterwards made the practice of collaboration in Venetian studios of the late 15th and early 16th centuries not the exception but the rule. If we know that both Giorgione and Titian are to be

found in certain pictures why not tell the world? It is extremely interesting since it is a firmly established fact. It is my contention that Giorgione painted portraits which Titian and Sebastiano were encouraged to emulate as part of their education. Thus, as we have already observed, the *Young Man* in Berlin led six years afterwards to the *Bearded Man* similarly dressed who correctly bears Titian's signature in London's National Gallery. Mr. Goldman's *Man with Hand on Book* was the model for the *La Schiavona* who must have been one of the earliest of Titian's sitters. And the *Knight of Malta*, more inimitable than it seemed, was the pattern picture for all the portraits of men by Titian up to 1520 and for other portraits by such followers as Sebastiano, Torbido, Palma, Cariani, Lotto, Catena, Pordenone, Licinio, Mancini, Romanino, and Savoldo.

The young Titian was of course by far the best of the lot. He was from the outset a professional portrait painter who saw heads and figures objectively and with an impersonal naturalism as well as with a taste for sumptuous decoration and the dignity of the great world. He and Cariani completed many of the canvasses which their close friend Palma left unfinished at his death and the three men were so much alike in mental outlook and technical ability that when they collaborated there was a successful fusion.[1] It was Titian's genius to carry to the nth degree of grandeur and of skill what is commonplace in the work of Palma and Cariani and in the taste of the average person. But when Titian worked reverently from the inspiration of Giorgione making at first his own unintentionally explicit imitations, or later touching up with naturalism the unfinished starts in his leader's studio, he did not set out to glorify the ordinary but to explain and to elaborate the extraordinary. It is eloquent of the creative power of Giorgione that he was only partially concealed. This has led to disputes about celebrated pictures; opinions differing according to whether the critic sees more of the leader's thought or more of the follower's touch. Never does it seem to have occurred to the authorities to stop the controversy and the frequent exchange of labels according to the shifting winds of prevailing influence, to stop it all with the simple and correct statement that the work in question is not by Giorgione *or* Titian but by Giorgione *and* Titian.

Titian was the perfect portrait painter. He studied the way the skin covers the bony structures of the skull. He studied the shapes of the eye sockets in their relation to the cheek bones and the nose. He analysed the expressiveness of the eyes, the lips and the chin. He observed the light playing over the surface of the skin. He penetrated to the ruling passion underneath but always with the good humour of a wise and tolerant man of the world. If he had a bias it was for life's more impressive aspects. He caught likenesses I am sure, but glossed over pettiness in his sitters and without the obvious flattery of the later court painters such as Van Dyke. And his brushwork performed miracles in the tactile representation of textures which Giorgione also had loved but which he, Titian, could render both with more dexterity and more illusion than his leader. There is no portrait entirely by Giorgione which can be compared in quality to the supremely fine *Man with Hat and Gloves* owned by Viscount Halifax in London and the famous *Man with Glove* in the Louvre.

And yet the *Knight of Malta* is something different, something which started Titian towards his finest portraits although more than a portrait itself. It has none of the qualities I have outlined as Titian's characteristics. It has a remote and mysterious glamour which Titian never knew how to capture, which he may never have even registered in his own mind. If by many good judges the *Knight of Malta* is included on their lists of

[1]The curious three figure composition in the Detroit Museum, a middle aged man between two women, is obviously the work of three painters. Titian certainly painted the blonde woman at the left. I suggest Cariani and Palma as his collaborators.

fer that he had carried memories and studies of them, having been close to his master when they were being planned and placed on canvas. He was still a student and was deliberately and intelligently assembling in his mind and imitating with his hand fragments which he liked not only in Giorgione but also in Dürer, Mantegna, Leonardo, Michelangelo, Raphael and Marcantonio. Lacking imaginative invention he had a compensating genius for assimilating design-elements which were adaptable to his own capacities and intentions. Unlike Giorgione he was always making drawings and his sketch books contained memories of the mountains, pastures and farm houses at Cadore and copies of figures from paintings and engravings. It was natural that during Giorgione's life his influence over Titian was but one of many, the greatest no doubt, but by no means the only admiration. After the tragic loss of his leader however the ambitious student and potential rival returned to the studio which had formed him and to the responsibility imposed upon him by fate in a mood of devoted discipleship. For several years he subordinated himself to the service of Giorgione.

I am confident that Titian was independent and entirely on his own initiative while in Padua. The beautiful colors of the frescoes in the medical school, especially the Miracle of the newborn baby, echo Giorgio's palette. There is a Giorgionesque contrast too of the arch with the long, straight, diagonal staff. But the lining up of the actors, as if on a stage, the realistic portrayal of the models employed, the back drop of the Roman statue, the weedy vegetation and the streaky sky all reveal a difference from the mature Giorgione of the rhythmical *Pastoral Music* and *Adulteress*

Before Christ, a difference which is even more marked than the deferential reference to those important works which he had seen only a year before while the Pastoral was in the making and the Adulteress merely begun. The resemblance of the lateral many-figure arrangement with a wall at one end and an opening at the other to the similar problem of the Adulteress at Glasgow has led many critics to the logical conclusion that Titian utilized the experience of the fresco to aid him in the actual execution of the similar but superior composition in oils. But although the Adulteress was finished after the Miracle of the Babe it was I feel sure started before the fresco. It was, as I see it, a studio experiment of 1510, undertaken and designed by Giorgione with Titian and Sebastiano in mind as the ultimate executants. Commissions for such subjects, uncongenial to the master himself, could be accepted on condition that they could be treated less as story or as spectacle than as commentary. The stormy incidents which occur at the barriers of life where passionate intolerance and passionate sympathy clash would not be merely melodramatic narrative if treated with a subjectively emotional atmosphere and with multilateral rhythms of interacting lines, tending to the ever desired quality of abstraction. But the master died before he had done much more than plan the picture and, after 1510, Titian returned to finish what he had helped begin and what probably had been designed for him even as the *Judgment of Solomon* (Bankes Collection) had been sketched in the studio for his own use in the fresco at Vicenza.

On his return to the workshop where he had learned his art Titian found the *Pastoral Music* all but finished and by far the best part of his inheritance. He did nothing to change its original and essential character. His discreet naturalistic touches in 1511 may arrest the eye with their concern about such non-essentials as detailed texture but the design remained unchanged. If glowing glazes were added as late as 1530 they only enriched the colors and enhanced the intensity inherent in the poetic theme. Glazes can make a color scale higher or lower in key than at its origin but if they leave the structure and design unaltered we have the same balance and relativity. The *Pastoral Music* is the essence of Giorgione's life-long intention and Titian recognized and respected it as such. Those of us who see traces of his mind and hand in the picture and who are willing to concede that it may possibly be the pastoral "with nudes" which he presented to Duke Frederic of Mantua in 1530 in delivering to his patron the *Madonna of the Rabbit*,[1] are only ready to believe that he had retouched it a little while before presentation and that he offered it not as his work but as his gift. It had been his most prized possession so long and had inspired him so intimately that he may not even have told the agent Malatesta that it was not his own creation. But the truth prevailed. When the great picture passed to King Louis XIV and later to the Louvre it was known and promptly catalogued as a Giorgione and it has done more to establish a universal appreciation of the true character of his art than the iconoclastic pedants have been able to undo. It is undeniable that in the Louvre one sees a resemblance in the glowing colors to the Titians of 1530 which came from the same collections. The explanation is that they were all given final glazes at about the same time and have all been varnished in the same institution.

But it is fortunate that whatever Titian may have done to his leader's masterpiece early or late while it was in his keeping, he did not transform it with his explicit and objective mentality. The bits of his surface retouching which have been mistaken for modern restoration must not mislead us into Hourticq's blunder of attributing to the young follower his leader's matured and mellowed masterpiece. It contains not only Giorgione's unique, intellectual and emotional subtleties but also evidences of his improvisation, that adventurous practice of drawing and correcting with the brush instead of following preliminary studies and sketches which gave to the Florentine Vasari in his life of Giorgio an excuse for a sermon on spontaneity achieved at too great a cost.

There is less of Titian in the *Pastoral Music* than in the *Sleeping Venus* and the Pitti *Concert* and far less than in the *Christ and Adulteress* and the *Madonnas* at Vienna and at Madrid. The *Gypsy Madonna* at Vienna is so much more coarsely painted than her sister at the Prado that I suspect the overpainting by Titian was executed when he was very young, perhaps as early as 1508. If it had not been for the revelation of the x-ray I might never have suspected that there was a lay-in by Giorgione underneath. In spite of the grand, pyramidal design and the wall and window arrangement and the striped curtain and the color scheme, all very like Giorgione, the heavy folds, granular surface and square brush stroke are, as I have said in an earlier chapter, completely Titian and the picture should be so labelled. But the little unfinished *Madonna with St. Anthony and St. Roch* in the Prado is a problem which I have not solved to my entire satisfaction. Its

[1] L. Hourticq "La Jeunesse de Titien," Ch. I, pp. 22-30.

Detail: MADONNA WITH SAINTS   PRADO, MADRID

GIORGIONE AND (OR) TITIAN

small size, its exquisite paint quality, the tiny flowers of the brocade behind the Virgin, the transparent shadows and the linear rhythms in the crisply crinkled draperies are as characteristic of Giorgione as the pensive, downcast eyes and oval face of the beautiful young mother. It has been brushed spontaneously and without a fault in sparkling jewelled colors. Titian had not yet reached such finesse in 1511. And yet Titian definitely comes to mind even in the Giorgionesque details. The Madonna's spiritual shyness has in it a conventional Praxitilian prettiness. That we can match S. Anthony and S. Roch with figures by Titian done while he was in Padua may only mean that he had seen the start by Giorgione in 1510 as he had seen the almost finished *Pastoral.*

Parts of this composition as of the other may have inspired him to respectful plagiarism while working alone on the frescoes and on the designs for the wood cuts. Nevertheless in this case I wonder whether Titian, shortly after his arrival in Venice in 1511-12, did not paint this picture in its entirety as a tribute and in as close an approximation to his lost leader's fully developed style as he could command. The "plague Saints," the book and the lily might then have some special meanings, as in the case of the St. Mark enthroned, at the Salute, which Titian painted on his return from Padua as a thanks offering for having survived the scourge. One can make one's own deductions. Was the religious picture now in Madrid Giorgione's last stand against the illness which killed him and was its inspirational haste in execution interrupted by death so that Titian revered it and left it as he found it or only a little less unfinished? Or was it Titian's own idea and his own execution in 1511 and discontinued by him lest he lose the Giorgionesque quality which up to that time he had preserved?

In any event it helped him to finish the *Sleeping Venus* a year or two later. The line between the lips of Venus he may have accentuated but the head is essentially as it had been since 1507 when the leader left this idyll to decorate the Fondaco. What he painted in 1511 or 1512 was the hill town and the white cloud over it and the Cupid which later was painted out but which the x-ray has located and the contours of which can still be seen when the thin canvas is placed against the light.

Earlier than Titian's work on the *Sleeping Venus* was his execution of the central portion of

ADULTERESS BEFORE CHRIST   GLASGOW   MADONNA & SAINTS   PRADO, MADRID

(Detail by Titian)   *(Detail by Titian)*

GIORGIONE AND TITIAN   GIORGIONE AND (OR) TITIAN

The young accuser of the Glasgow Adulteress has an obvious resemblance of pose to the S. Roch of the Madonna at Madrid and both figures were probably executed by Titian in 1511 after having done a similar young man in the Fresco of the Miracle of the Babe at Padua. This does not mean however that Giorgione may not have planned and drawn the fragments here illustrated before his death in 1510

the unfinished *Christ and Adulteress* of Glasgow. All of the early references in old documents confirm my belief that it originated with Giorgione. I can only assume however that it was a commission in which he meant to collaborate with one or both of his associates. There are two versions extant and a copy of one of them by Cariani at Bergamo. A studio project is clearly suggested. Seventeenth century writers mention pictures representing the subject by Giorgione in the collections of Michele Spietra and of the brothers Pesaro. In the inventory of the collection of the Swedish Queen Christina there was an Adulteress with the same attribution. A letter, published in 1757, from Livio Meo to Ciro Ferri bears an allusion to the question as to whether Giorgione or Titian painted a picture on the same theme which was then in Florence. In the Art Bulletin for September, 1934, G. M. Richter's article on Unfinished Pictures by Giorgione, in referring the student to the above citations, expresses the writer's opinion that the conception and composition could not have originated with either Sebastiano or Titian, to both of whom it has been attributed, although the actual execution points to one or the other, at least in part. But "none of their known works of 1510 show such a rhythmic and spirited unification. They are all of a more statuesque type." "If Giorgione had any part in the execution," writes Richter, "it was at the left where the soldier with his back turned to us and the person with the golden chain may well have been painted by Giorgione himself." I agree. Vasari told of Giorgione's special interest as a virtuoso in reflecting surfaces and mentioned several pictures he had painted of men in armour. Even more clearly his than the figures

at the left is the transparent shadow on the wall back of them and in the space between—a passage of marvelous painting which anticipates the tonal and aerial subtleties of Rembrandt, Vermeer and Chardin. Certainly that corner of the picture in Glasgow contains Giorgione's crackle and his thin and fluid brush work. But all over the length and breadth of the canvas there is abundant evidence of his originality and of his genius for imagining moments when men and women are not only affected by but revealed in fateful incidents for which he was able to find equivalents of rhythmical arabesque and colorful light. Christ's compassion for the sinner and his scorn for her hypocritical accusers are conveyed in an impulsive gesture in which his restraining hand saves a hunted creature from the pack by an action as impulsive as it is innate. Stirred to involuntary and incoherent movement these men and their victim are seen in a room which opens at one end to a serene, sunny meadow. The enclosure needs that glimpse of air and space for its lights seem charged with the colors of overheated human passions.

The painting in Glasgow was mutilated at an unknown date by the cutting off of a strip of canvas. Those who criticise the composition would not do so if they knew what had happened to spoil the creator's intention. Fortunately the operation was not fatal to the fascination of the picture. From Cariani's copy at Bergamo we know that a tall bearded man who, in the design, had served as the column at the right end of the shallow semicircle balancing the man in armour at the left, was removed, no one knows when or why. As a result of his removal the skirt of the Adulteress had to be repainted and it looks like a 17th century job. I learn that Queen Christina of Sweden had a way of adding to or subtracting from her pictures to make them fit into places in her palace. The picture in Glasgow which suffered this mutilation must have been the *Adulteress Before Christ* which is listed in the catalogue of her collection and as a Giorgione. Not long ago the missing man was discovered and identified by Mr. Berenson who congratulated the unknown vandal on having detached the best figure of the group for separate enjoyment. The fragment is now a self-sufficient painting of attractive dimensions in the distinguished collection of Mr. Arthur Sachs. Before I saw this delightful upper right hand corner of the Glasgow Adulteress in Mr. Sachs' apartment in Paris I had studied the photograph of his treasure and been reminded of the Raphaelesque inclinations of Sebastiano. Incidentally the sandalled foot of the Christ in Glasgow resembled the foot of the youngest of the *Three Wise Men* and might have been an attempt to repeat that earlier success in overpainting a detail of his master's drawing. Could he have assisted Giorgione in starting the Adulteress and painted the handsome personage at the right who functioned so prominently in the pattern, just before he left for Rome to join the following of Raphael? If so, Titian, on his return from Padua, might have had this terminal figure by his former associate cut away so that all that remained to be done from left to right, the Adulteress, her young tormentor and the others, would be entirely his. But my first glimpse of "the missing man" who appears to be a handsome man about town, convinced me that only Giorgione could have conceived his self-concealing and revealing facial expression, his side-

"THE MISSING MAN"   ARTHUR SACHS COLLECTION
(*Fragment from Adulteress Before Christ*)
GIORGIONE

long look as of one concerned with what the world would say about his undignified part in an embarrassing incident. The beauty and delicacy of the brushwork, the glimmer of the gold threads on the green-black of the man's coat, the harmony of this area with the ruddy flesh tones and with the chestnut brown of the adjacent man's shoulder as well as with the blue of the hills and the silver of the sky proclaimed a great colorist. The variety and swing of the silhouette from the line of light edging the three-cornered cap, worn at a jaunty angle, down the strong column of the neck to the shoulder in a sweeping curve revealed the master of decorative and plastic contours. The figure as a whole was a unit of design in Giorgione's most decorative manner and the face revealed his subtle generalized characterization. I am now convinced that he painted this man at the extreme right end of the Glasgow picture and the landscape and sky beyond his grandly silhouetted form. I am no less sure he painted the two figures at the opposite end and the shadowed space behind them. Interested chiefly in the structural and ornamental function of these two literally outstanding figures, the missing man and the warrior in armour, he filled in the corners and their backgrounds and then turned over the balance of his project to his junior partners. It was their task, first Sebastiano's and after the chief's death, Titian's, to work from the two ends in towards the turbulent center. Dr. A. L. Mayer is one of several authorities who agree with me that the Sachs fragment is the work of Giorgione. Its exquisite technic reminds him of the *Madonna* at Madrid which he also attributes to the leader instead of to the follower. The majority opinion agrees with Berenson in giving the missing man, as well as the composition from which it was cut, to Titian in 1511.

I am inclined to think that the beautiful portrait privately owned in London of a *Young Man with Hat and Gloves*, his gloved hand resting on a parapet, the portrait which was long known as "the Temple Newsam Titian" may have been at least started by Giorgione in 1510.[1] At that time he had developed, as the copy of the strong head at Brunswick testifies, a more fluid quality in his paint and a broader, more detailed and less detached observation of life and character. When we come upon supremely fine portraits of 1510-12 which reveal solicitous inter-pretations of lyric truth and psychological insight but also a degree of realism in the modelling and in the surface painting of skin and varied textures, then we have reason to suspect that Titian finished what Giorgione had begun before he died. It has been our custom in recent years to call the most subtle and sensitive of the young Titian's portraits Giorgionesque instead of suggesting that they may have been not merely inspired by but actually conceived and designed by Giorgione himself. Our thought has been almost spiritualistic. The master's penetration to the inner life of his sitters is supposed to have passed into Titian's possession as a legacy. From a better world Giorgione is imagined as guiding Titian's hand when he painted such a masterpiece as the *Young Man*, now in Lord Halifax's house in Piccadilly. It deserves to rank with the *Physician Parma* in Vienna and the Louvre *Man with Glove* as one of the greatest of all portraits. It achieves a plastic existence which is fairly pulsing with life and it draws out of the eyes an admission of a sorrow or a secret locked deep in the recesses of an intellectual and patrician reserve. The mystery which was beyond Titian is blended in this fine presence with the suave brushwork and the accurate record of the individual's physical self which had been, in earlier years, beyond Giorgione, or at least outside of his self-limited scope. Since I believe so strongly that Giorgione was more inventive and imaginative than Titian, more sensitive and subtle in design, more spark-

[1]Lionelli Venturi assigned it to Palma because of its resemblance of soft modelling and of background details to his portraits of men in the National Gallery, London, and the Querini Stampalia, Venice. I agree with Berenson that Palma imitated this portrait but that Titian executed it.

PORTRAIT OF MAN WITH HAT AND GLOVES   VISCOUNT HALIFAX, LONDON
TITIAN

The finest example of the art of Titian lifted to a higher plane under the influence of Giorgione who may have conceived and underpainted the portrait

ling in touch and more elusive in suggestion, then I am glad to balance that belief with the acknowledgment that Titian was the better portrait painter. The marvelous reproductive skill with which the *Young Man* in London is painted makes Giorgione's tender lyrical truth underneath more convincing than if he himself had lived to veil it with his subjective mood or to make it the symbol and epitome of an idea.

The great Giorgione Pastoral in the Louvre is the culmination of a series of successive efforts to convey personal conceptions through a language of colorful design. In this masterpiece better than ever before he attained to a subtly satisfying organization of interlocking parts and crossed diagonals, of verticals and long, slow sweeping curves, of ponderable figures artfully persuaded into postures where their contours function in a persistent rhythmical pattern. His ecstacy over this achievement of a musical self-sufficiency intensifies our delights in the intellectual elements involved, in the reconciliation of opposites, of edges fused in softly rounded masses, of solids in space, of golds against blue, of light enchanted scarlets, browns and greens, an excitement of oppositions resolved with vibrant harmonies.

The most distinguished exemplars of the four distinct kinds of art criticism assume that the *Concert Champêtre* was the work of Giorgione. On the strength of their assumption we rank him as one of the supreme artists of the ages. The way of Walter Pater[1] was the way of aesthetic contemplation as an inspiration to poetic prose. His critical perception was as sound as if he had not striven chiefly for literary enchantment. Pater noted the beginnings of skep-

tical research on the subject yet remained unperturbed in his confidence that the painter of the two Concerts of Florence and Paris was either Giorgione or an Anonimo of equal genius and the same mentality and character. The man of genius, whatever his name, was the first painter to make the evanescent accidents in the visible world a source book of constant reference in pictorial self-expression. As the observer of exquisite moments when lines, lights and colors seem to be one with music Giorgione required from Pater a tribute of cadenced subtleties of phrasing and delicate felicities of suggestion. Into the scholar's style as he wrote there came a glamour similar to his theme. An afternoon glow would seem to have been woven into the texture of his words with the same gold threads Giorgione used for his urban and sylvan music makers, his oak groves and his sheep pastures. A drowsy spell pervades the senses as we read; a mood is captured like the painter's own nostalgia for the passing hour, his passion for the present moment. As in the great picture in Paris which so greatly inspired him we are made aware of lights that fade and waters that fall, of pleasure's overflow, of sweetness run to waste, of life that is too short a dream. Such a transcript of lyric painting into lyric prose was imaginative interpretation in terms of sensibility.

The second way to the subject, a development from Pater, teaches the rhythms of history, the alternations of synthesis and analysis, of collective functionalism under communal faith gradually replaced in the recurrent cycles by that emancipated individualism which, in the Ren-

[1]Walter Pater, Essay on "The School of Giorgione" in "The Renaissance."

aissance, extended from the patrons of art to the artists themselves, not merely tolerating but actually luxuriating in their varied, personal reactions to environment and experience. Elie Faure,[1] the philosophical historian, has written of Giorgione that he was the first to paint, in the *Pastoral Music*, a true symphony; color, line, light and form all inseparable and interrelated, the painter's own mood analysed and converted into a unified plastic symbol.

The third critic studies a picture from the purely technical point of view, evaluates what it means to be plastic on a flat surface. Giorgione, in the words of Albert C. Barnes,[2] "led the way to the structural use of color combined with light in an all pervasive color-atmosphere which unified the inner organizations of line and mass" . . . "He is the one man whose richness of plastic values makes him a serious rival of Giotto for the highest place in the hierarchy of art" . . . "His color functions in design to the greatest extent to which color is capable of functioning" . . . "In the *Concert Champêtre* the eye cannot rest anywhere without finding the fullest satisfaction." All this from a difficult and exclusive disciplinarian and anatomist of design who discounts charm in art, requiring what he calls "a legitimate foundation for poetry in painting" and no less for its enjoyment by the observer.

The fourth kind of critic is the expert and archivist. He is apt to be beset with doubts which gather over his judgment as he weighs the evidence in the old records and uses alternately the methods of the research scholar, the detective and the psychologist. I wrote to Bernhard Berenson asking him if Titian, as Giorgione's exe-

cutor, had not gone over the *Pastoral* of the Louvre at different times. I saw his coruscating touch in the golden red garment of the lute player which interrupts with its opulence the travel of the eye over the perfect pattern. Berenson replied as follows: "When I saw the painting in full daylight its superiority to anything Titian was doing at the time became at once manifest." He urged me to set my mind at rest on whatever Titian may have added. Giorgione conceived, designed and executed the *Concert Champêtre* in 1510. The Titian of a later year may be found on the surface but Giorgione alone is there both in spirit and in substance. What the disciple may have done is unimportant. That he did something is obvious. Fortunately it was not much. "There is" and now I quote Berenson again, "a touch of heavy rusticity in everything Titian painted up to 1530—always excepting the portraits." Thus the best of all the four kinds of critic are certain that the Louvre is correct in not changing the attribution of their greatest Italian treasure in spite of the pressure brought upon it to do just that by the French critic Louis Hourticq and those other pan-Titianists like Suida who agree with him.

Hourticq has both small and large reasons for thinking that Titian painted the *Concert Champêtre*.[3] There is a boy's face under curly hair in a fresco at Padua and another one engraved in the Triumph of Faith, both very like the tousled blonde head of the shepherd in our Concert of

[1] Elie Faure—Renaissance Art, Harper Bros., 1923, p. 182. The Spirit of the Forms, 1930, p. 46.

[2] Albert C. Barnes, "The Art in Painting," Barnes Foundation Press, 1925, pp. 174-5.

[3] Louis Hourticq, "La Jeunesse de Titien," Ch. 1.

DRAWING OF A SEATED WOMAN *copied from Giorgione's*
PASTORAL MUSIC
MALCOLM COLLECTION, BRITISH MUSEUM
TITIAN

the Fields, the lad who blends his reeds with the lute of the city man by his side. And there is a drawing in the Malcolm Collection, (of the British Museum), possibly a study for a lost painting, where we are startled to find the seated girl of the Louvre *Pastoral*, the very one who has her back turned to us and her right knee drawn up to prolong the diagonal line of her left leg and her flute. The pose is identical in the drawing and the plump little model has the same small head and sloping shoulders. I can only repeat that Titian at this time was taking what he wanted for his own use from the great painters he admired and filling his note books with drawings not only from life but from art. Hourticq's observation that the landscape background of the Malcolm drawing contains Titian's mountain at Cadore, the Marmarole, and sheep like those which graze and sleep in the sunny meadows of the painting, illustrates the point perfectly. The

drawing is a frank borrowing by Titian of one of the figures in Giorgione's masterpiece. This he combined with his memories of the Alpine background of his childhood.

I have stressed the point that the young Titian from 1507 to 1512, first as the apprentice on the frescoes in Venice and finally in completing his leader's unfinished works as his executor, was proudly imitative of Giorgione. After 1512 he tried a pastoralism on his own account which is very attractive but very different. The Allegory at Bridgewater House with the rural lovers— what a contrast it is to the *Thunderstorm* and its family group! It is a contrast of the mind of an average man with the mind of an evasive but entrancing poet. One feels the difference again in comparing the lovely profile of Giorgione's earth woman at the well in the *Pastoral Music*, her deep shadowed eyes, sensitive lips and softly rounded contours, as plastic and generalized as a fine Greek coin, with what Titian derived from it in his own taste for his Venus in the Borghese Palace as she leans towards her blonde and bland client with professional advice. The lovely face of the goddess in that masterpiece of symmetrical decoration is that of a gorgeous model showing one side of her classic features. The profile is chiselled with a grace derived from the Greeks but from an academic light and leading.

The larger reason for Hourticq's dispute with the traditional and all but universal attribution of the *Pastoral Music* to Giorgione has already been referred to in the chapter on "what we learn from Michiel and Vasari." But his deduction from Michiel's list needs to be repeated in order to be again refuted. He jumps to the conclusion that since the *Three Philosophers* was left un-

Detail of STANDING WOMAN: PASTORAL MUSIC   LOUVRE, PARIS
GIORGIONE

Detail of VENUS: ADVICE OF VENUS   BORGHESE PALACE, ROME
TITIAN

We feel the difference between Titian and Giorgione in details such as the outlines of two heads. Compare the lovely profile of Giorgio's earth woman at the well, her deep shadowed eyes and softly rounded contours, as plastic and generalized as a Greek coin with Titian's Venus—a sumptuous model showing one side of her classic features

finished in 1510, then that was the sort of work he must have been doing up to the end. He could never then have achieved a High Renaissance breadth, could not even have started the *Sleeping Venus* which Michiel reported as merely finished by Titian. The x-ray has now silenced this argument with its proof that the *Three Wise Men* was an early work, its underpainting dating from about 1500. Now it is indisputable that the documented Giorgiones and the never questioned *Madonna* at Castelfranco all reveal a poet painter of fresh vision and a keen observer of landscape under expressive conditions of light but not a powerful realist and neither Ruskin's "fiery heart to Venice" nor even Vasari's Venetian Leonardo. They give no clear assurance that their maker would become a painter of large figures well modelled in light and shade, and of an epicurean pantheism more persuasive even than Titian's Bacchanals. The Zanetti engravings however show the transition to greater plastic power and confirm Vasari's statement of the change which occurred in his style in 1507 resulting in what became well known as a "fuoco Giorgionesco." The difference between the hedonist philosophies of the two men is that Titian was of the world as well as in it. Giorgione only enjoyed his contemplation of the physical from "where the blue begins," from the so called "pathos of distance," from the poet's and from the painter's point of view. His blithe and contented detachment avoided both the obviousness of facts and the disillusionment of worldliness. His preference for the role of spectator and his zeal for the art of painting as an end in itself merged with a high hearted sensuousness but also with a high minded idealism.

That Pastoral at the Louvre which marks an epoch and which anticipates conscious romanticism and color construction in modern painting, what else does it all mean? Only perhaps the music we improvise at picnics, the fun an artist has with his lute out in the fields, his friends in the latest fashions, the pipes of Pan and shepherd songs of a simpler age, the sun browned flesh of country girls close to the soil, their little classic heads, the great groves of old trees in late summer splendour, the last caressing gleams of evening light and far away the blue shadowed mountains. It is all quite dream-like and incongruously assembled. The forthright mind of Titian would have made a good story out of it. The imagination of Giorgione converts its sensuous imagery into a universal poem in praise of peace and all the golden afternoons that ever were, when the heart is light even as the shadows lengthen, when, in idleness and with no vain regrets, loving time as it flies, drinking deep of the light while it lingers, for yet another tranced moment we know the warmth of the sun before it sinks and all the mellow generosity of the earth.

The autograph *Thunderstorm* of the Academia was the first landscape to evoke such a mood. In the *Pastoral Concert* the mood is very different of course but no less subjective and compelling. We are lured to the sunny slopes of Arcady. There is no excitement anywhere, not even in the flash of sunlight on the distant sea nor in the swing of the old trees against the sky. Exhilaration itself is steeped in a relaxed ecstasy. The impromptu concert for the eye is accompanied by the soundless music of imagined sheep bells far down in the lowland pastures and by the thought of water falling from the crystal pitcher at the well to complete our sense of well being. Instead of the tense and cryptic storm we have a contrasted mood in which all cares and troubles cease. The critic W. Suida who, in his book on Titian, follows Hourticq in fairly consistent agreement, confesses himself unable to understand how the same man could have expressed such antithetical states of mind as are revealed in these two landscapes. He asserted that Giorgione was an introvert who could only have painted fantasy and haunting visions. That *Thunderstorm* at Castelfranco anticipated El Greco's *Storm Over Toledo!* In both pictures there is an all-over pattern, in both a weird light. The two young people and a baby seen by Giorgio as if in a lightning flash, so exposed to the storm and yet so indifferent to the menacing elements, they were of course a dreamer's hallucination. How could the artist have changed so much in seven years that he could paint the care-free pastoralism of the picture in Paris? To this there is only one answer. Being what he was, a man of impressionable and mercurial temperament, how could he have failed to change under serene influences of environment and happy experience? The storm of his youth foretold the golden glow of his maturity.

All his life he had been painting the emotion which evades expression and yet which has to be expressed. He did not sign his canvases with his name but with a unique spirit and a unique language of functional design. No other artist can be mistaken for him if we come to understand the man and his special gifts and limitations. His closest associates followed his methods for a while and even participated in or added finishing touches to his projects yet without sharing the subtleties of his thought. He valued their intimacy and their aid and assisted them to develop their capacities of a different kind. Unfortunately he did not protect his nectar from their adulteration. Critics like Hourticq and Suida have paid too little attention to Giorgione's consistent guidance of his own constantly evolving style. It was certain that he would change, that a mellowness and a strengthening form would have to be found for a maturing and a deepening substance. The poetry of the earlier Giorgio had to grow older and wiser, less self-withdrawn, more confident of power and purpose, more expressive of profound thought, more at peace with the world. His insistence from first to last on the important role of pattern in a lyric picture led him in a few years of swift progress from promise to perfection. An ever increasing receptivity to new methods of expression and to ripened reactions from experience resulted inevitably in the *Pastoral Music* and its dream of physical sublimation and of peace at the glowing heart of nature.

The "Autograph" Giorgione

The one work which is not only documented but entirely by his own hand

TEMPESTA: "THUNDERSTORM AT CASTELFRANCO"   ACADEMIA, VENICE

Detail of TEMPESTA: FIGURE OF MAN

Detail of TEMPESTA: FIGURE OF YOUNG WOMAN

Detail of TEMPESTA: STORMY LANDSCAPE AT CASTELFRANCO

"Surely by Giorgione"

This list includes details he painted for pictures not completely his and important works finished by assistants either before or after his death

FIRE ORDEAL OF MOSES   UFFIZI, FLORENCE

PASTORAL MUSIC

Attributed to Giorgione

Paintings which, for many different reasons, are here credited to him at least in part; but the critics are not unanimous in agreement

ADORATION OF THE SHEPHERDS   LORD ALLENDALE, LONDON

The design and landscape by Giorgione but the group in front of the cave by a pupil of Bellini borrowed for the purpose

MAN WITH HAND ON BOOK   GOLDMAN COLLECTION, NEW YORK

Berenson and Lionello Venturi assign this fine portrait to Titian but the facial expression, intense with
suggestion of inward conflict, and the structural simplification of the forms are eloquent of Giorgione

Detail: BUST OF WOMAN AGAINST LAUREL LEAVES   VIENNA

According to the authentic inscription this face was retouched by Giorgione in 1506. It is here suggested that the picture was begun by an unknown painter and repainted with alterations by Romanino

{ 115 }

ANTONIO BROCARDO   BUDAPEST

An original by Giorgione, finished and altered by another hand

PORTRAIT OF ARIOSTO?   METROPOLITAN MUSEUM

Finishing touches may have been added by Titian

BUST OF YOUNG WOMAN   LORD DUVEEN

*The exaggerated expression and prominence of
the eye reveals retouching by another hand*

JUDGMENT OF SOLOMON   BANKES COLLECTION, KINGSTON-LACY

*By Giorgione and his Junior Partners. A project of Giorgione's studio for a fresco which was
later executed by Titian. The unfinished figures at the right seem to have been laid in by Giorgione*

SHEPHERD BOY WITH FLUTE   HAMPTON COURT

Detail of Boy: THREE AGES   PITTI PALACE, FLORENCE

This head from the THREE AGES *in spite of its repainted condition suggests that it originated with Giorgione. The painting as a whole may be described as a product of the studios of Giorgione and the late Bellini*

"THE MISSING MAN"   SACHS COLLECTION

From extreme right of the Glasgow Adulteress by Giorgione himself

{ 126 }

MADONNA WITH SS. ROCH AND ANTHONY   PRADO, MADRID

*Either Giorgione's last picture left unfinished at his death in 1510 or a successful
imitation by Titian in 1511-12 painted in reverent tribute to his lost leader*

{ 127 }

Supplementary Illustrations

Paintings which include Juvenilia and Copies of Lost Originals by Giorgione, Paintings from the Studios of Bellini and Giorgione, and some Important Works by their Followers, including Titian

ALLEGORY OF THE TREE OF LIFE

UFFIZI, FLORENCE

BELLINI

One of the most probable sources of Giorgione's inspiration at the formative period of his life

JUDGMENT OF SOLOMON UFFIZI, FLORENCE

SCHOOL OF BELLINI

Only the landscape by Giorgione, the figures by a less gifted fellow-pupil of Bellini

ALLEGORICAL IDYLL (HOMAGE TO A POET)   LONDON, NATIONAL GALLERY
SCHOOL OF BELLINI
Close to Giorgione

SOLDIER AND YOUNG MOTHER   MARQUIS OF
IN LANDSCAPE   NORTHAMPTON
STUDIO OF GIORGIONE
Ruined and badly repainted

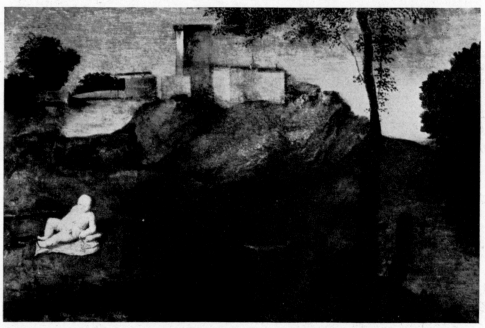

PARIS EXPOSED   FRANK JEWETT MATHER, JR.
SCHOOL OF GIORGIONE
Perhaps a copy of a Lost Giorgione by Dosso Dossi or Romanino

AENEAS AND ANCHISES   PRESENT OWNERSHIP UNKNOWN

STUDIO OF GIORGIONE

c. 1503. A ruin which has been completely repainted. It may have been
an original by the master and the picture of Aeneas listed by Michiel

PORTRAIT OF A LADY WITH HANDKERCHIEF   BORGHESE PALACE, ROME

*Copy of a lost Giorgione. Morelli and Berenson consider
it a ruined original. The copyist may have taken liberties*

S. SINIBALDO   S. BARTOLOMEO DI RIALTO, VENICE   S. LODOVICO   S. BARTOLOMEO DI RIALTO, VENICE

SEBASTIANO DEL PIOMBO 1507   SEBASTIANO DEL PIOMBO 1507

Note the influence of Bellini and his illusion of figures standing in semi-circular
niches in shadowed light. Sebastiano was a recent graduate from Bellini's school

JOHN CHRYSOSTOM AND OTHER SAINTS   S. GIOVANNI CRISOSTOMO, VENICE

SEBASTIANO DEL PIOMBO

This picture was probably planned by Giorgione to be executed by his assistant

ZANETTI ENGRAVING OF   FONDACO DEI TEDESCHI,
TITIAN FRESCO   VENICE

TITIAN 1507-08

Note the resemblance of the angel to the frescoed faces

TOBIAS AND THE ANGEL   SANTA CATERINA, VENICE

TITIAN 1507

MADONNA OF THE   JULES BACHE COLLECTION, NEW YORK
TREE TRUNK   TITIAN

HOLY FAMILY   MARQUIS OF BATH COLLECTION
                              TITIAN

MADONNA AND CHILD IN LANDSCAPE

Probably Cariani's copy of a lost collaboration by Giorgione and Titian.
The design is worthy of Giorgione and can be attributed to him

TITIAN

Over a start by Giorgione

GYPSY MADONNA

LADY WITH LEFT HAND ON PARAPET   COOK COLLECTION

TITIAN

TITIAN

JARVIS COLLECTION, YALE UNIVERSITY

A damaged sketch from the studio of Giorgione

MADONNA AND CHILD · BELLINI 1510 · BRERA, MILAN

TESTIMONY OF THE NEW BORN BABE (*Fresco*)　　TITIAN 1511

SCUOLA DEL SANTO, PADUA

{ 154 }

BOY WITH ARROW   VIENNA

TITIAN?

Copy of a lost Giorgione

PORTRAIT OF A BARBERIGO?   NATIONAL GALLERY, LONDON

TITIAN

The quilted sleeve and the signature indicate a late repainting

CUPID ON A BALUSTRADE   ACADEMIA, VIENNA

TITIAN
Copy of a lost sketch ?

PORTRAIT OF MAN WITH RED CAP AND FURS   FRICK COLLECTION, NEW YORK

TITIAN

NOLI ME TANGERE   NATIONAL GALLERY, LONDON

TITIAN

THE ADVICE OF VENUS

TITIAN

BORGHESE PALACE, ROME

(Better known as SACRED AND PROFANE LOVE)

{ 160 }

Detail: THE ADVICE OF VENUS   BORGHESE, ROME   *Detail:* MADONNA AND SAINTS   VIENNA

TITIAN   TITIAN

Clothed Woman   *St. Ulphus*

Examples of the young Titian's achievement of mastery in 1512-14. The waning influence of Giorgione and the growing friendship with Palma combine to make him conscious of his own maturity

PHYSICIAN PARMA   VIENNA

TITIAN

One of the latest manifestations of Giorgione's inspiring influence
over Titian and one of the greatest works of his early maturity

PORTRAIT OF A MAN   HAMPTON COURT

TITIAN

BUST OF WOMAN AGAINST LAUREL LEAVES   VIENNA
UNKNOWN ARTIST
In part by Giorgione 1506, repainted with changes by Romanino

THREE AGES

PITTI PALACE, FLORENCE

STUDIO OF GIORGIONE?

Variant on a lost Giorgione referred to by Vasari: conceivably begun by the master (The Boy), finished by Bellini or Catena or both 1511

ST. JEROME WITH SS.   CHURCH OF
CHRISTOPHER AND AUGUSTINE   SAN GIOVANNI CRISOSTOMO
BELLINI 1513
Note the influence of Titian

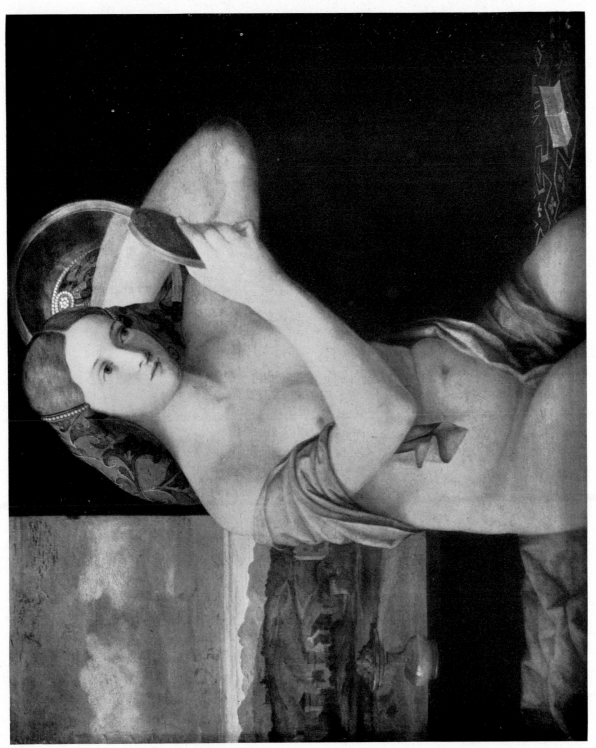

BELLINI 1515

YOUNG LADY DRESSING HER HAIR

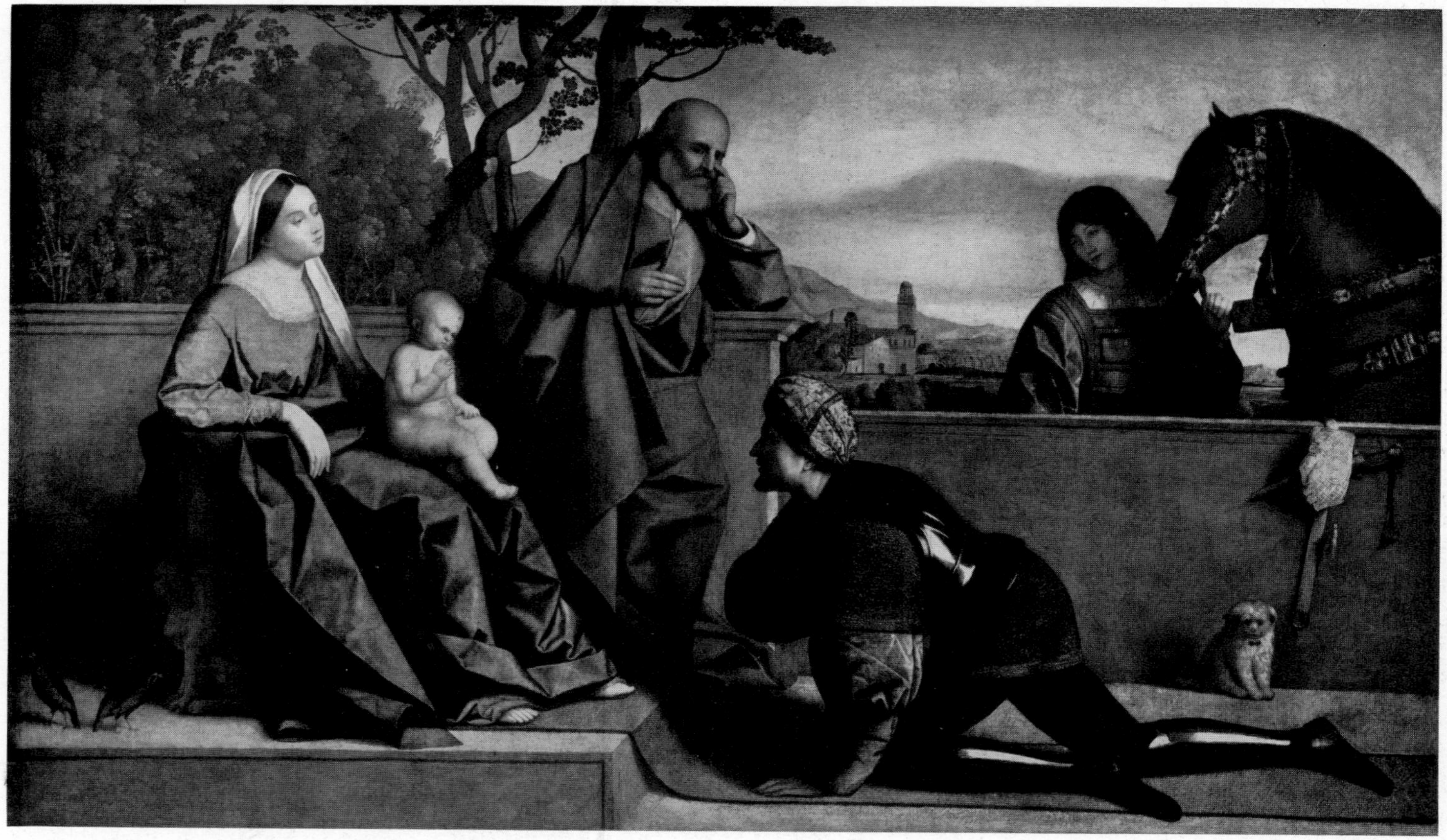

WARRIOR ADORING INFANT CHRIST — NATIONAL GALLERY, LONDON

CATENA

Berenson, in his Venetian Paintings in America, p. 244, referred to Catena's hesitating and retarded yet truly appreciative response to the influence of Giorgione. He had "one of those minds over which the old and the new exercise the same fascination, and this drew to him the admiration of like-minded eclectics, such as the humanists Bembo and Marcantonio Michiel." The masterpiece in London reveals the combined influences of the last period of Bellini and the Giorgionesque romanticism

PORTRAIT OF A POET   NATIONAL GALLERY, LONDON

PALMA VECCHIO

JACOB AND RACHEL   PALMA VECCHIO   DRESDEN

The pastoral of Giorgione has been adapted by Palma for mass production and consumption.
The realism and the lavish abundance of color and interest show the inevitable end of the episode

VIOLINIST   ROTHSCHILD COLLECTION, PARIS
                    SEBASTIANO DEL PIOMBO
            Giorgione's influence has been combined with that of Raphael

Venetian Paintings

Not illustrated but mentioned in the text as related to the background-studio or influence of Giorgione. This List is suggestive, not comprehensive. It is a cross-section of the Giorgionesque

The copy at Budapest of a portion of Giorgione's lost BIRTH OF PARIS. *The original was seen by Michiel in the house of Taddeo Contarini and mentioned as an early work. The two shepherds at Budapest are identified as a fragment by reference to the engraving of Th. von Kessel. Illustrated opposite page 46, Herbert Cook's Giorgione and on page 14, Martin Conway's Giorgione as a Landscape Painter.*

Tenier's Copy of Giorgione's BIRTH OF PARIS *which is in the collection of Mrs. Loeser in Florence. It is illustrated opposite page 17, Martin Conway's Giorgione.*

Small Panels representing THE FINDING OF PARIS. *Collection of Lord Conway, Allington Castle. These pictures may be described as Venetian folk painting at the end of the 15th century. Because we know from Michiel that Giorgio painted this subject in his boyhood it is possible that the little panels show his juvenile efforts in or near Castelfranco before 1494.*

The ORPHEUS *of the Widener Collection has been attributed to Bellini by Berenson and others and is illustrated as his work in Paintings at Lynnewood Hall, page 164. Possibly painted for Isabella, Duchess of Mantua, who persisted in her efforts to get him to paint classical allegories.*

Lorenzo Lotto's earliest Giorgionesque pictures are rare and fascinating. I need only mention his ST. JEROME *in a sylvan landscape, described and illustrated (page 55) by Thomas Munro in Great Pictures in Europe, and dated as early as 1500 by Berenson, and his* DANAE *owned by Lord Conway and illustrated plate* cxxxi *in the catalogue of the Burlington House Italian Exhibition of 1930.*

Palma Vecchio's HALBERDIER, WOMAN AND BABIES IN LANDSCAPE *from the Wilstach Collection, Memorial Hall, Philadelphia, is illustrated in one of the Pennsylvania Museum catalogues. The late Mr. Babbott of Brooklyn owned a similar imitation of Giorgione by Palma.*

Cariani's RAPE OF HELEN *in the Metropolitan Museum is illustrated on page 39 of Berenson I Pittori Italiani, 1936. It is a product of the School of Bellini and shows the influence of the young Giorgione and of Carpaccio.*

The Vienna copy (by Titian?) of Giorgione's ADORATION OF THE SHEPHERDS *in Lord Allendale's Collection. It is in the magazine of the Vienna Gallery. Illustrated opposite page 20 in Herbert Cook's Giorgione.*

Catena's ADORATION OF THE SHEPHERDS, *formerly in the collection of Lord Brownlow, reveals the fusion of colors in light and the romantic pastoralism which this artist gleaned from the later Bellini and Giorgione.*

ST. EUSTACE *attributed to Titian and illustrated as his by Suida in his book, plate* cccva.

Titian's CUPID AND VENUS *in landscape of the Wallace Collection, London, Suida plate* cccvb.

Titian's DOUBLE PORTRAIT OF TWO MEN, *Berlin, Kaiser Friederich Museum. Illustrated, plate* xxvii *Suida's Titian. It has been suggested that it may be a copy of Giorgione's Borgherini* BOY AND HIS TUTOR *mentioned by Vasari.*

MADONNA WITH SS. CATHERINE AND SEBASTIAN *in the Louvre (illustrated, Herbert Cook's Giorgione, page 104) is by Sebastiano.*

Unknown Artist, Venetian School, PORTRAIT OF AN OLD WOMAN, *Academia, Venice. Attributed to Giorgione by Berenson who however is almost alone in this opinion. The anonymous artist reveals familiarity with Giorgione's decorative style and his mannerisms but his realistic intention is unlike anything we know of the master. The picture has seldom if ever been reproduced in books but good photographs can be purchased at the Academia.*

Another Giorgionesque item at the Academy is the documented TEMPESTA DI MARE *now acknowledged to be a collaboration of Palma and Paris Bordone. Plate xliv, Lionello Venturi's Giorgione e il Giorgionismo.*

At Vicenza (Museo Civico) there is a PORTRAIT OF A BEARDED YOUNG MAN *attributed variously to Giorgione, Titian, Lotto and Licinio. Illustrated, page 362 in Ferriguto's Giorgione.*

In the Detroit Museum there is an obvious collaboration of three painters on the picture of a MAN BETWEEN TWO WOMEN. *The buxom blonde at the left is by Titian and I attribute the man to Cariani and the beauty at the right with the Greek profile to Palma.*

In the Querini Stampalia, Venice, is found a PORTRAIT *by Palma which Herbert Cook erroneously attributed to Giorgione, illustrated in Cook, page 84.*

In Suida's book on Titian attention is invited to plate ccxxb. AN OLD MAN PRAYING *is evidently a donor cut away from an altar painting. Berenson attributes the fragment to Pordenone.*

Bonifazio Veronese in his youth is credited by Berenson with the VENUS AND ADONIS, *National Gallery No. 1123, which is illustrated as a Giorgione in Cook, page 94.*

In Suida's book on Titian, plate lviii, both a and b are Giorgionesque but (a) IL BRAVO *is by Palma, possibly a copy of a lost Giorgione, and* (b) BOY WITH TAMBOURINE *is an early Paolo Veronese.*

List of Giorgione's Pictures

Cited by Marcantonio Michiel ("L'Anonimo") as being
in his day (1525-75) in private possession at Venice

Casa Taddeo Contarini (1525)

1. THE THREE PHILOSOPHERS
   (*Identified as* THE THREE WISE MEN *in the
   Vienna Gallery*)

2. AENEAS AND ANCHISES IN HADES
   (*Possibly the large landscape with an old
   man and boy recently discovered in Venice in delle Rose Collection*)

3. BIRTH OF PARIS
   (*Identified by the engraving of Th. von
   Kessel. A copy of the part representing
   the two shepherds is at Budapest*)

Casa Jeronimo Marcello (1525)

1. PORTRAIT OF M. JERONIMO ARMED, SHOWING
   HIS BACK AND TURNING HIS HEAD
   (*This reference strengthens the hypothesis
   that Giorgione painted the similar figure
   in the Adulteress at Glasgow*)

2. A NUDE VENUS IN A LANDSCAPE WITH CUPID
   FINISHED BY TITIAN
   (*Identified as the Dresden Venus*)

3. S. JEROME READING

Casa M. Anton. Venier (1528)

A SOLDIER ARMED TO THE WAIST

Casa G. Vendramin (1530)

1. LANDSCAPE WITH SOLDIER AND GYPSY
   (*Identified as the* THUNDERSTORM AT CAS-
   TELFRANCO *in the Academia, Venice*)

2. THE DEAD CHRIST ON THE TOMB, SUPPORTED
   BY ONE ANGEL
   RETOUCHED BY TITIAN

Casa Zuane Ram (1531)

1. A YOUTH, HALF LENGTH, HOLDING AN ARROW
   (*Probably the* EROS *or* BOY WITH ARROWS
   *in Vienna is a copy or studio variant
   from this lost original*)

2. HEAD OF A SHEPHERD BOY, WHO HOLDS A
   FLUTE
   (*The Head at Hampton Court*)

Casa A. Pasqualino

1. COPY OF NO. 1 JUST MENTIONED
   (*This might be the copy in Vienna*)

2. HEAD OF S. JAMES, WITH PILGRIM STAFF
   (*Or, may be, a Copy*)

Casa Andrea Odoni (1532)

S. JEROME, NUDE, SEATED IN A DESERT BY
MOONLIGHT
COPY AFTER GIORGIONE

Casa Michiel Contarini (1543)

A PEN DRAWING OF A NUDE FIGURE IN A
LANDSCAPE
   *The painting of the same subject belonged
   to the Anonimo*

Casa Piero Servio (1575)

PORTRAIT OF HIS FATHER

*It is noteworthy that two of the above pieces are cited
as copies, from which we may infer that Giorgione's pro-
ductions were already, at this early date, enjoying such
a vogue as to call for their multiplication at the hands of
others, and we can readily understand how, in course of
time, the fabrication of "Giorgiones" became a profitable
business.*

Note by Herbert Cook in the Appendix to his GIORGIONE, 1907.

Bibliography

Archivio Storico dell'Arte, by A. Luzio, Archivist of Mantua, 1888.

Marcantonio Michiel (L'Anonimo di Morelli): "Notizie d'opere del disegno" by Jacopo Morelli, 1800; 2d edition by Gustavo Frizzoni, 1884.

Vasari's Lives of the Painters:
First edition 1550; Second edition 1568. English translation by Mrs. J. Foster, 1850; used by Blashfield and Hopkins in their edition of Vasari's Lives, 1896.
Edition G. Milanesi, Florence, 1881.

Lodovico Dolce: "Dialogo della Pittura, intitolato L'Aretino," 1557.

Carlo Ridolfi: Le Maraviglie dell arte della Pittura, 1648.

David Teniers: Le Theatre des Peintures, Antwerp, 1673.

Nadal Melchiori: Cronaca di Castelfranco, 1724-35, Museo Civico di Venezia, Cod. Gradenigo-Dolfin, 205.

Anton Maria Zanetti: Varie Pitture a Fresco, de principali Maestri Veneziani, mdcclx.

Anton Maria Zanetti: Della Pittura Veneziana e della Opere Publiche de Veneziana Maestri, mdcclxxi.

Giovanni Morelli (Ivan Lermolieff): Italian Painters, 1893, 2 vols.

Herbert Cook: Giorgione, Bell & Sons, London, 1907.

Ludwig Justi: Giorgione, Berlin, 1908, 2 vols.

Charles Ricketts: Titian, Methuen & Co., 1910.

G. Gronau: Giorgione, Berlin-Stuttgart, 1911.

Lionello Venturi: Giorgione e il Giorgionismo, Milan, 1913.

Lionello Venturi, Italian Paintings in America, E. Weyhe, 1933.

Bernhard Berenson: Italian Painters of the Renaissance and List of Works, Oxford Press, Revised edition, 1930.

Bernhard Berenson: Venetian Paintings in America, F. F. Sherman, New York, 1916.

Bernhard Berenson: I Pittori Italiani del Rinascimento, Milan, 1936.

Louis Hourticq: La Jeunesse de Titien, Librarie Hachette, Paris, 1919.

Louis Hourticq: Le Probleme de Giorgione, Librarie Hachette, 1930.

Sir Martin Conway: Giorgione as a Landscape Painter, London, 1929.

Frank Jewett Mather, Jr.: History of Italian Painting, Holt, 1923.

Frank Jewett Mather, Jr.: Venetian Painters, Holt, 1936.

George Martin Richter: Unfinished Pictures, Art Bulletin, September, 1934.

George Martin Richter: A Clue to Giorgione's Late Style, Burlington Magazine, March, 1932.

Johannes Wilde: Röntgenaufnahmen der Drei Philosophen Giorgiones und der Zigeunermadonna Tizians. Jahrbuch Kunst Samml. n.s. 6:141-52, 1932.

W. Suida: Le Titien, A. Weber, Paris, 1935.

Arnaldo Ferriguto: Attraverso i "misteri" di Giorgione, 1933.

Walter Pater: The Renaissance, Macmillan Co., 1910.

Elie Faure: Renaissance Art, translated by Walter Pach, 1923.

Elie Faure: The Spirit of the Forms, translated by Walter Pach, 1930.

Albert C. Barnes: The Art in Painting, Barnes Press, 1925.

Raimond Van Marle: Italian Schools of Painting, M. Nijhoff, The Hague, 1935, 27 vols.